Movement of New African Leaders

Movement of New African Leaders

Seddoh Bokor

Published by Seddoh Bokor, 2024.

While every precaution has been taken in the preparation of this book, the publisher assumes no responsibility for errors or omissions, or for damages resulting from the use of the information contained herein.

MOVEMENT OF NEW AFRICAN LEADERS

First edition. August 12, 2024.

Copyright © 2024 Seddoh Bokor.

ISBN: 979-8227195340

Written by Seddoh Bokor.

Also by Seddoh Bokor

1

The Second Betrayal of Jesus Christ

The Second Betrayal of Jesus Christ

Standalone

Movement of New African Leaders

Seddoh Bokor

Address: P.O. Box DT 2752, Adenta, Greater Accra Region, Ghana

E-mail: sebokor@live.com

Table of Contents

Chapter 1 : Being Yourself 8

Dedication

This book is for the new generation of African leaders who are prepared and ready to chart a new path in the substance of the African Personality. A big shout-out to Mr Nana Kwame Bediako, a businessman, philanthropist, and the Leader of the New Force - a political movement to renew leadership in Ghana and across Africa.

Much appreciation goes to President Bassirou Diomaye Faye, the youngest President in the history of Senegal for his courage to stand and be elected in 2024 as the leader of his country.

In retrospect, the book appreciates the morally upright and selfless African leaders, politicians, traditional leaders, and others who, for the love of their fellows, sacrificed for political power and showed the pathway to economic empowerment.

["We are sitting on a gold mine but looking for gold from other places."]
Nana Kwame Bediako, 2024

Acknowledgement

This book appreciates the reviewers, designers, and technicians who worked around the clock to the end. Importantly, it gives thanks to the reader in the hope that you will find some lessons that you could use to improve the quality of life of people.

Preface

The effects of set minds and practices are not exclusive to individuals but can belie the dynamism of institutions, especially political establishments. In such moments, the inauguration of something new brings bewilderment and possible opposition to change. Nonetheless, the change comes to stay. This is what this book is about.

Chapter One identifies, among others, the African leadership problem to be the lack of adequate preparation, moral discipline, and experience and their effects on the leadership character since independence. It expresses the dangers ahead if the trend is allowed to continue. It makes suggestions about the pragmatic ways to reverse the situation.

In Chapter Two, the book focuses on application of experience to win deals for improvement in living standards on the continent. It is presented against the background that although Africa contributes more than 30% of the world's resources, it gets less in return because leaders enter into bad contracts.

Chapter Three examines the general framework within which the African leader functions. It examines the historical, political, administrative and economic trajectory and their impacts. It contrasts this situation with the European systems, extolling the dangers of implanting foreign political, administrative, and economic systems. One of the positions of the book is that such foreign systems are more understandable to the educated African than the masses who still connect with the original African governance systems.

Chapter Four elaborates on the functionality of multi-party democracy on the continent. It looks at the value systems in contrast with the African identity and asks, "Is multi-party democracy the only answer to unity in development for Africa?"

Chapter Five proposes actions African leaders should take to address critical socio-economic and politico-administrative challenges.

It recommends, among others mobilization of African talents within and outside the continent, and an integrated inter-continental policy especially on trade and natural resources.

Chapter Six examines the moral courage needed by the Neo-African leader to achieve and set exemplary standards for the next generation. It brings to the fore a gamut of challenges that are inter-linked in the process of political decision making and execution.

In the various chapters, the book brings out relevant quotes and actions to support the point that leadership is not just about talk but action; the creation of opportunities, motivation and mobilization of people to perform at their highest levels.

NB: In the context of this Book, "He" is used to represent every gender.

CHAPTER ONE

Being Yourself

*["We will no longer accept politicians who are all talk and no action –
constantly complaining but never doing anything about it. The time for
empty talk is over. Now arrives the hour of action. Do not let anyone tell
you it cannot be done"]*

Donald J. Trump, 2017

In June 2015, Donald John Trump announced his Presidential ambition as a nominee for the Republican Party in a rare gallant manner adorned with a stylish descent of the staircase in Trump Towers, New York. For many people in and outside of the USA, 'The Donald's attempt to enter into an established institution like the US political system was not worth paying any attention to because his records as a "Master Estate Developer," showed that he did not belong there.

"The Establishment" that bolstered its relevance on the democratic axiom of "government of the people, for the people, by the people" has over the years built a wall around itself which insulates it from the very people it seeks to serve, not for the lack of noble democratic aspirations but by the cumulative misconducts of the political class. And for this situation to exist, ideologies somehow share similarities; to find gaps and plough the system, set normative patterns of comportment and promote certain standards called "political correctness" or "looking presidential."

More importantly, "The Establishment" has its path for achieving political greatness, the recognition that for a Johnny-come-lately, his family must be well-connected in high places, and without doubt, should be seen to have a trace of political chronicles. So when 'The Donald' declared his ambition to wrestle power and ascend to the highest political office, it was received by various classes of people in different ways.

There were those who accepted him with doubts and also those who ignored him. There was also a class of people who laughed it off sarcastically and others who swore to oppose him. There was a sense of wonder and disbelief in many other people (including the writer) as to why a billionaire would take such a risky step when all indications were that he was not of the same conventional politically correct stalk.

Indeed, 'The Donald's decision begged comprehension, so many people simply resigned themselves with the remark "Let Trump be Trump". Even when he won the nomination of the Republican Party, not much of the uncomplimentary views about him changed. Rather, he was scoffed and tagged as a firebrand. Even when some polls showed it was possible for him to pull a surprise, many people paid little attention.

So it was until the count of Electoral College votes in the wee hours of 8th November 2016 that "Trump indeed became Trump" - the 45th President of the United States of America, and by so doing, an overwhelming ambition got fulfilled.

Like it or not, admire him or not, the bottom line was that the deal was struck democratically between him and the American people, and the effects rippled throughout the world. Why?

Many factors come to play. World leaders, by snowballing have over the years piled upon themselves systems of regimented political practices that eventually tend to insulate them from their peoples. They fail to keep up the connection. In such moments of superficial political correctness, the patterns and processes become so ingrained and uncompromising that many people forget that human institutions are not sacrosanct. In its gradual descent into irrelevance, the political system exuded compulsion, blazing like a crusading monster that sought to make all fall in line without regard to that essence in the human being that cries for things even beyond political freedom. No matter the political system, be it in Asia, Africa, America, Europe, Russia, or wherever, it cannot be vouchsafed that as a human institution, it is so perfect that it has no defect. So when such set practices become drossy and demotivation for progress, time has a way of fixing the system, and it does so through an inspired individual or a group of people.

So Trump came to the USA in 2016, with an ambition and a message that resonated so well with those who felt "down there;" for whom government works no more –and they guaranteed the Electoral College victory for the 'Donald'. He came as a businessman par excellence and promised a government that will not be there to manage competing political interests in only high places but bring the citizens into the mainstream national development agenda, for whom government must work again, harness and harvest their talents for a decent and happy life. This message is profound and should touch the deep recesses of leaders across the world and especially the people in developing countries so-called. If a super power like the USA can experience a change of reawakening to that magnitude then there should be useful lessons for all.

The Anguish of African Leadership

The danger facing many African democracies today and possibly in the future is the inadequate preparation of people who hold or aspire to hold political office. Such people seem to have only the desire but have failed or are failing to work sufficiently in translating it to achievable ambition over time. To lead people to attain not only political independence but economic empowerment and to give them the requisite enablement for the realization of their dreams is a serious matter. It is not a prank and charlatans ought to stay away. It should be genuinely pursued by people who thirst to be at the service of their fellow sisters and brothers without priority concern for self. This is what governance is about; to produce tangible results by significantly meeting the material and aspirational needs of the people.

The celebration of independence days across Africa is a politically worthy exercise. However, it should not supersede the urgency for leaders to take critical decisions that will lift up people, and provide them with food, shelter, health, education, et cetera so that they live decent lives and exhibit their God-given talents. Otherwise, what is worthy about celebrating an independence when the majority of the people are impoverished but their leaders live in opulence?

History shows that in the development of human societies, meeting the material needs of life is a significant trigger for security and a reason to win social recognition hence, such achievers are called "wealthy people." To own material things has long been the source of inspiration, struggle, power, and the means for those who have to dominate the "have nots." For whatever reason, society continues to recognize and reward possessors of materiality. Until humanity grows out of this, it will remain a fact that material possessions are good bets for fame, power, and popularity.

The records show that many African leaders make their wealth when they assume leadership roles and seek to deploy their "questionable" prosperity to win more power, fame, and love from innocent citizens. This situation was said to be more profound in many autocratic regimes in the early post-independence period. The theorists touted Western democracy as the way to go; to protect citizens from the high levels of resource plunder. Has the answer been found in democratic governance so far? Not yet, because the state arrangement has not sufficiently empowered the African Public Management/ Administration system; it is weak, dominated, and virtually in the throes of ravaging political leaders who have a strong appetite for materiality. They have not developed sufficiently to (i) insulate themselves from undue political interference (ii) remain a distinct, non-partisan tool for the execution of policies (iii) serve as the means for securing state resources against partisan political vagaries.

When these weaknesses are looked at from the prevailing cultural beliefs, attitudes, values, and non-assertiveness of the people (who seem to "tolerate" the plundering of state resources), a lacuna is observed that becomes the enablement for African leaders to prevail against state arrangement and infringe on the sovereignty of citizens.

Unmistakably, anybody who sees his political position as a gateway to wealth creation for himself, family, cronies and ethnic group, is regrettably wrong and does not understand the purpose of life and the human development trajectory. Historically, the legacy of effective leaders was not built on a quick-win. It came from overarching values, diligence, and commitment to lift the majority of people from oppression, poverty, and ignorance.

It stands to reason that effective leadership requires some life-long journey; to experience the highs and lows across various strands and compasses. And in the process, and as opportunities naturally come, translate desire into ambition. It is important for the individual to do so if he wants to master the art of being himself to become successful in life.

Often, desire is the incentive for action; it comes as an urge, fluidic, and sparks good thoughts and feelings. Sometimes, depending on its impelling force, it gives a picture of the expected changed state. But because it is unstable, it requires efforts to concentrate and transform it into achievable plans and actions. It means one must be focused and work assiduously to realize an ambition. The more often this is done, the more personal and cosmic energy is released to drive the desire. Discipline is required (by being focused, generating and reinforcing thoughts and actions) to achieve an ambition with persistence and time.

Mr Donald Trump has a track record in life and wealth creation. He has the desire and ambition – to identify the trophy (set target), to be disciplined about how he gets it, and remain focused. The educational qualification or geographical location plays little role in setting an ambition. Each person has his level and incentive. What matters is to be capable of rational thought and right action. In this regard, it is necessary to tap into one's personal strengths (if recognized) in combination with the opportunities granted by nature.

There are stories about people coming from poor family backgrounds who became world-acclaimed models of leadership while others who were born into rich families became failures in life. The fact that one is born into a well-to-do family, or the delusional belief of belonging to a superior race, ethnic group, or whatever, is no guarantee of a successful delivery on ambition or vice versa.

Nonetheless, the more conducive the environment is, the more the paths to realizing the ambition. For example, it will be a useless ambition for a Democrat to seek candidature in a one-party socialist state that does not believe in multi-party election just as the same will be said of a hardline Socialist assimilating and vying for a position in a multi-party democratic state. The ambition that seeks to effect a change in any of those political systems is highly exceptional and over tasking. So ambition counts, and taking time to prepare through experience gathering, will eventually yield results. That is why African leaders should appreciate that the fight for political freedom ended several years ago, and the new one at hand is how to provide the necessities of life for their citizens.

Unlike the contest against a physically present colonial master, today's struggle is subtle and strategic that requires a high level of intelligence, state organizing principles, ownership building, commitment, and being results-focused all of the time. The fight is amidst a historical antecedent in which the interest of the colonial masters and other foreign powers is unending. It is as strong today as the day Vasco da Gama set sail with the motive of merchandise.

The African Ordeal

The world has never seen in its annals a region that suffered unfettered colonization to the magnitude of Africa. It is a continent whose innocence became ignorance and whose resources became a target for appropriation by colonial masters from the past to the present day. The historical books affirmed that France, the United Kingdom (then England), Germany, Italy, Spain, Portugal, and Belgium have had and continue to have their lion's share. China, Russia, India, Japan, et cetera are also having a bite now. In attestation, they built partnership agreements, associations, and unions under the pretext of creating a win-win situation. Love was shown to Africa for the love of her resources.

Even when Africans in the 1950s through the 60s went through a continental struggle to free themselves for something somehow called "independence," events today show that it is but the opening of a new chapter of a bigger "fight" in which the African will not have to fight only his colonial master but also, his own fellow African Leader. The material things that should provide the enablement for Africans to lead a decent life are vastly "controlled" by external forces. Over 30% of the world's resources come from the continent but Africans are not winning to rise above the afflictions of disease, illiteracy, hunger, housing deficit, lack of access to quality water, and poor sanitation. The continent seems to host the downsides of life. What accounts for this situation? How can it be changed?

African leaders are struggling to master themselves and win deals. They are failing to design and pursue homegrown governance and development strategies. Tactical thinkers are in short supply in the face of a superficial colonial educational system whose fundamentals of "knowledge devoid of results-based practice" remains unchanged in many countries.

Multi-party democracy is the order of the day but can only get good as the character of those who practice it. Many African leaders are still struggling to internalize its tenets. For now their leadership and orientation in life might not necessarily be different from those of the past military leaders – which sounds like you are either with the ruling government and prevail in life or oppose and perish.

The period of military interventions showed Africans what should not be done because it failed to chart a collective path to progress, and most of the military heroes changed over to lead civilian governments. But should the military adventurers be blamed? Not necessarily because many African leaders betrayed the noble ideals of democracy and equaled or became worse than some military dictators. They were undisciplined, corrupt, power-drunk, divisive, unaccountable and egoistic.

The African democracy is yet to rise above intolerance, and the destructive system of "winner takes all." The contribution of the opposition party to add value to the governance process is perceived as a hazard. Thus roadblocks are mounted to prevent it from a possible win of power in the future.

Similarly, power-drunk leaders fail to concede elections for another person to continue the arduous task of nation-building. They are oblivious to the fact that the strategic human resource of a nation is not exclusive to themselves or the ruling party. The examples include Ivory Coast (2008), Gambia (2016), and Democratic Republic of Congo (2016). There are, however, good practices from Nigeria (2015), Benin (2016), and Ghana (2016).

Many African leaders have yet to appreciate that political leadership is a selfless act but not a means for honing wealth. Since they fail to appreciate its sacrificial part, the exhortation to deploy good governance to impact livelihood will be defeated, and people will continue to suffer from the lack of quality health, education, shelter, job opportunities, and improved living standards. This deprivation does not provide the enabling environment for people to develop their God-given talents towards a happy life. They see the government as having failed to work for them; the State has ceased to watch their backs, and they have been left behind to be on their own.

Trump - Manifestation of an Ambition

The records show that Mr Donald Trump was born on 14th June 1946, into a family that could be said to be relatively wealthy. At the age of 70 years, he won the Presidency to become one of the oldest US Presidents. He went through the vicissitudes of life that led to the experience he gathered over the years. As a young graduate, he took over the estate development business of the family and turned it around within the shortest possible time. The lesson here is that value addition should be paramount to the art of being oneself. To keep sticking with the status quo undermines progress, because transformation matters. The effort at renewal is key to progress in life – to be ahead of others and set examples worth emulation. It is doable if we scan our environment to identify the factors that shore us up.

How we navigate the pros and cons of each and aggregate environmental factors coupled with the action taken will shape our success or setback. Win or lose the experience is the basis for self-renewal. The point is that at a stage of self-development- to become oneself - there are many seemingly negative things that one can transmute into positive things. Success will not always climax every action. No! Far from that. There will be painful losses, but one must learn the resultant lessons and apply them diligently when the next opportunity comes. We can look at how "The Donald" in business sense, set a debt of $916 million in 1995 against the legal provision and got cushioned for 18 years or so from paying federal tax. Did he break the law? Time will tell. He demonstrated a classic case of due diligence, astuteness, and the drive to turn things around in life. No situation is so bad as not to leave a window of opportunity. It means that to master the art of being yourself, you must transform from being a dreamer or/ and theorist to becoming a fearless practitioner. By practicing you will understand the dynamics of change and how to adapt. The ultimate is about people, to meet a need and it is by experience that one can empathize and lend a helping hand.

Formal education sharpens our motor, cognitive and affective modes and facilitates intelligent analysis. One cannot make a meaningful headway without having a critical mind. It does not mean we should be psychoanalysts. No! We should be capable of thinking rationally in the abstract, to weigh alternatives and taking the right decisions coupled with the courage to reduce risks.

Mr Donald Trump completed graduate school and had a degree in Economics in 1968. Straightaway one can see the link between an educational certificate and the career path. He has an added advantage because his career has a foundation in the family's estate development business.

Many programs and courses are still dominant in the curricula of African educational institutions dating back to the colonial days. Regrettably, these courses become the last resort or forced on students without considering their interests and aspirations. Worse of all, they are theoretical and irrelevant to the priority needs of industry. Many graduates are not well prepared for the job market by way of exposure and the development of a winning mentality. So rather than booming with self-confidence and a can-do attitude, the African youth harbors an inferiority complex even before taking the first step in life after school.

Education should not only seek to develop the psycho-motor-affective nature; importantly it should connect the person to his environment with the skills required for initiative, work and earning a decent livelihood. In any case, what does psycho-motor-affective mean to the unemployed, the hungry, the homeless, and the forgotten? Almost nothing and anybody in this situation will probably live by fleeting desires without any focus to translate them into ambition. Living by desires alone does not support anyone to master the art of being himself. The congruence in education, personality and career enables the individual to strive for achievement, to keep dreaming, doing and experiencing life in varied ways.

Wikipedia.org succinctly described the case of Mr Donald Trump as,

["*In 1971 he took control of his family[1]'s real estate and construction firm, Elizabeth Trump & Son, which was later renamed The Trump Organization[2]. During his career[3], Trump has built, renovated or managed numerous office towers, hotels, casinos and golf courses. Various other products and activities[4] bear his name. He owned the Miss USA[5] and Miss Universe[6] pageants from 1996 to 2015, and has made cameo appearances[7] in films and television series. From 2004 to 2015, Trump hosted and co-produced The Apprentice[8], a reality television series on NBC[9]. As of 2016, he was listed by Forbes[10] as the 324th wealthiest person in the world[11], and 113th in the United States, with a net worth of $4.5 billion.*"]

Being multi-talented and multi-skilled is a natural flow in the process of maturity. It is like a formula for solving the challenges of life. Many of them have semblances, and by the diligent application of the acquired knowledge and skills backed by the right attitude, the individual becomes successful. Malaria in East Africa is not different from malaria in West Africa. The same prescription by the doctor is

---

1.   *https://en.wikipedia.org/wiki/Family_of_Donald_Trump*

2.   *https://en.wikipedia.org/wiki/The_Trump_Organization*

3.   *https://en.wikipedia.org/wiki/Business_career_of_Donald_Trump*

4.   *https://en.wikipedia.org/wiki/List_of_things_named_after_Donald_Trump*

5.   *https://en.wikipedia.org/wiki/Miss_USA*

6.   *https://en.wikipedia.org/wiki/Miss_Universe*

7.   *https://en.wikipedia.org/wiki/Filmography_of_Donald_Trump*

8.   *https://en.wikipedia.org/wiki/The_Apprentice_%28U.S._TV_series%29*

9.   *https://en.wikipedia.org/wiki/NBC*

10.   *https://en.wikipedia.org/wiki/Forbes*

11.   *https://en.wikipedia.org/wiki/The_World%27s_Billionaires*

likely going to work. So, Mr Donald Trump applied the formula and chalked success in estate development, reality TV shows, marketing, beauty pageant events, authorship, and politics. But these ventures, especially politics come with a higher level of risk.

There are many on reaching the pinnacle of material achievement, become enslaved by the very assets they toiled to make; they are afraid to venture into new fields and sorrowfully remain unsatisfied about life because something in them yearns for that next exertion, something new which they cringe to inaugurate in their lives. They have all the wealth but remain unsatisfied. Yes, their wealth gives them some public recognition, power, and influence, but within, there is the urge for that "something new." They nurture new desires but are unable to translate them into ambition. They are too weak to venture; they reflect and say, "I am too old to do something new," but in their hearts, they know that that "something new" is knocking and gnawing. They hardly appreciate that their potentials supersede their evanescent wealth.

All over the world, leaders live on the contributions of the masses; from kingdoms to monarchies, from autocracies to democracies, they have overtly or covertly benefitted in various forms; power, wealth, love, and fame. Many of them, after leaving office forfeit the nice accolades accorded them, and from there, find it difficult to walk through life with confidence because they failed to master the "art of being themselves." It is, therefore, an incredible feat for a wealthy man like 'The Donald' to try something new and get elected as the President of the United States.

The dent in post-independence African leadership is the appropriation of state resources by the leaders who won elections democratically and promised their citizens (by an oath during swearing-in ceremonies) to work in trust for them. How soon do they forget their commitment and become "intoxicated" with the resources they command? From South to Central Africa and from East to West Africa, one government takes over from the other, riding on the back of the accusation it leveled against the other that "They are corrupt, Change!" only to find itself removed by another on the same charge, and the cycle continues.

The records go like this; 1. Democratic Republic of Congo: (1965–1997)-over $5 billion appropriated, 2. Nigeria: (1993–1998) - roughly $2-5 billion appropriated, 3. Chad under Idris Deby- $30 million appropriated, 4. Guinea- in 1998 gold mine worth billions of dollars was sold to a foreign country for personal gain, 5. South Africa- in 2016 millions of dollars were appropriated for the leader's comfort, 6. Zimbabwe (2018) - over US$5bn worth of diamonds allegedly could not be accounted for, 7. Ghana (2017) - over US$5bn allegedly could not be traced from gold exports to UAE. The list goes on and on and on. There is hardly any African government that is not afflicted by the malady of corruption. The irrational leadership quest for fleeting material things is primarily the bane of the economic independence of Africans.

It is not too difficult to identify such corrupt leaders. They

i. have some characteristics that give them away despite their cunning attempts to hide their ill-gotten wealth from the people;

ii. become rich overnight but we know it takes time to create wealth.

iii. are filthy rich, and thankfully, renowned media houses and investigative journalists are there to blow the whistle.

iv. try to cover up by saving in foreign countries under disguise – for instance, using others to front for them, and for this purpose, they are obsessed with off-shore financial institutions.

v. pay lip service to the issues of corruption and stage-manage investigations into the corrupt practices of their governments.

vi. try to manipulate the legal and electioneering processes (laws, institutions, and people) to perpetuate their ill-tainted regimes.

vii. resist leaving power even when their party lost elections democratically. By their conduct, many African leaders make a mockery of the continent's political independence.

viii. enter into poorly crafted contracts with foreign governments, financial institutions, and corporate bodies while thinking more about the percentage that will roll into their bank accounts than what works for the people.

ix. keep away from public scrutiny the terms of the contracts that they have entered into. Sometimes their conscience pricks them, but to give themselves some reprieve, they coin terminologies such as "Finder's Fees" or "Contract Negotiation Fees" or "Appearance Fees" and interpolate figures. For the fear of transparency and accountability, they

x. prefer dealing with foreign companies to indigenous businesses with the excuse that local companies do not have the capacity to deliver. Granted that indeed it is the case, what is more enabling than for a government to build the capacity of African enterprises; to make them more competitive on the world stage? Even a country as powerful as the US stresses the need to continue to develop American enterprises and make them more competitive in the global market. To this end, 'The Donald' mentioned a few things worth paying attention to at the World Economic Forum in Davos in 2018. The opening paragraphs of his speech run like this;

["I am here today to represent the interests of the American People, and to affirm America's friendship and partnership in building a better world. Like all nations represented at this forum, America hopes for a future in which everyone can prosper, and every child can grow up free from violence,

poverty, and fear. Over the past year, we have made extraordinary strides in the United States.

We are lifting up forgotten communities, creating exciting new opportunities, and helping every American find their path to the American Dream—the dream of a great job, a safe home, and a better life for their children. After years of stagnation, the United States is once again experiencing strong economic growth. The stock market is smashing one record after another, and has added more than $7 trillion in new wealth since my election.

Consumer confidence, business confidence, and manufacturing confidence are the highest they have been in decades. Since my election, we've created 2.4 million jobs. Small business optimism is at an all-time high. New unemployment claims are near the lowest we've seen in almost half a century. African American unemployment has reached the lowest rate EVER RECORDED in the United States. So has unemployment among Hispanic Americans. The world is witnessing the resurgence of a strong and prosperous America.

I am here to deliver a simple message: There has never been a better time to hire, to build, to invest and to grow in the United States. AMERICA IS OPEN FOR BUSINESS AND WE ARE COMPETITIVE ONCE AGAIN."]

Material things are important because they confer some physical security and comfort but cannot make anyone master the art of being himself. How much more if they are possessed by stealing from the people? Potentials are "bigger" than ambition. So, if the ambition of an African leader is to make a lot of money while in office, then he is a failure and has not mastered himself.

So many leaders performed so badly; they (i) were ill-prepared, (ii) did not understand the African history and development challenges, and (iii) had no strategic or workable plans that add value to lifting up Africa. Some simply did not have the potential to lead but by twist of fate, found themselves in such a position and eventually wasted the people's time, energy, and resources. They became a burden to their countrymen and women. After leaving office, they rued at the missed opportunities (if they cared to retrospect) and wished they had not been there or not taken certain decisions and actions. Well, it is just human?

The art of being oneself requires the individual to be sensitive to others, live for them, attend to their needs (not only physical needs), and leave them to judge how well he has performed. It is a tedious journey that demands patience, knowledge, care, and resilience. These factors make a demand on leadership for which reason those who tow the conservative line of political correctness are unfit because they live by the "cool" norm that becomes bare and stale at the end. They have never swum against the tide so they cannot tell how it feels aside from what they know by default.

Every individual has a potential, yet fear prevents us from taking bold steps toward fulfillment. Do we all have the same potential? No! We should, therefore, support those with leadership traits and are striving to assume higher responsibilities. At the right time, God-sent opportunities will come for them to serve the people impartially, equitably, in truth and love. So Trump came to America at the appointed time to chart a new path towards progress and prosperity and make government work for the people again.

CHAPTER TWO

Winning Deals

Ignorance is not a virtue for winning deals. It should be appreciated that knowing how to win a deal is part of the experience-gathering process, and inexperienced leaders cannot get big wins for themselves and their countries. That is why individuals and people who aspire to be leaders should thoroughly introspect and establish their capacity, what they need, what they put on the table, and its value against what they receive in return. They have got to be ready to compete with others within and outside of their countries to get the best for their people.

So as we go through life, the qualities we gather become the resources to deploy to identify opportunities, priorities, and support systems and how they collectively fit into a winning formula for a deal. We may win some and lose others along the way, but the loss does not matter as such; it strengthens us if we learn the lessons, develop the right attitudes, and prepare ourselves for the next opportunity. It takes an experienced dealmaker to detect defects in a deal, and call for a change. 'The Donald' during the Presidential race mentioned some deals that were not in the interest of the USA.

Examples are;

a. the Transpacific Trade Partnership (TPP) that brought together 12 countries into a free trade area. It was the biggest trade arrangement ever made after the World Trade Organization. "The Donald" discerned that the US was not winning the TPP deal big enough, so he would not ratify it. This decision was in disregard of the efforts of the previous administration to maintain TPP. He wanted higher concessions for the US from the trade partners such as Mexico, Chile, Australia, Brunei, Canada, Japan, Malaysia, New Zealand, Peru, Singapore, and Vietnam.

b. he took the same position against the Transatlantic Trade & Investment Partnership - or TTIP - with the European Union. Here again, "The Donald" was astute to identify its harmful effects on American industry, jobs and people in the long-run.

c. he rejected the North American Free Trade Area (NAFTA) to prevent American manufacturing jobs from moving to other countries. The Donald's irrevocable position was to compel co-signatories in the deal to accede to what was in America's interest first, then theirs could also be considered. He knows and is proud of his country's strength and will not settle for anything that is not commensurate regardless of the status of the parties. That is sturdiness of character.

d. the total denunciation of the 2015 Iran Nuclear Deal

e. loosening the post-financial crisis banking rule otherwise known as the 'Dodd-Frank Act'.

In welcoming the leader of Nigeria (the second sub-Saharan African leader after South Africa on assumption of his presidency) to the White House on 30th April, 2018 the US President mentioned the need for Nigeria to remove trade barriers and create a level playing field. The essence was to enable US businesses to invest heavily in the country.

Trump talks tough and is sometimes elusive with his real intentions in a bargain. He makes general statements and leaves his competitor guessing what could be his trump card. But he knows what he wants out of the deal. His abstraction, no doubt, is a sure way of dismantling the defenses of the competitor and preventing him from marshaling forces to win against him. It is like a coach in a football match who detected that the opposing side has well-gifted players who are not playing to any particular tactical formation for him to read and counter. Or better still, the team is so well-prepared that every player can attack, defend, scheme, and, importantly, score goals at every opportunity. Indeed, it will be a herculean task to overcome such a football team.

Trump gave indication of his elusive identity during the Presidential debate when the Democrats and their presidential candidate kept saying, "We do not know which Trump will show up at the debate." That is the trade mark of a vintage deal maker with many colors.

In Africa, signing bad deals in the past may be considered less grievous than the failure of new leaders to detect that such contracts exist and that there is a need to take steps to renegotiate them. Often, they (the leaders) could not take the trouble to unearth them, and the same mistakes recur. Ex-President Olusegun Obasanjo of Nigeria admonished African leaders at the 2017 Tana Forum in Ethiopia to increase their vigilance and negotiation skills to maximize the gains that would accrue to their citizens, especially in the mining and oil sectors.

While the individual can be excused for making some losses in deal-making, the same should not be the case for African Leadership because too many lives, craving for urgent development, are at stake and should not be ignored. The lack of self-confidence, insufficient knowledge, weak preparation, and bad judgment cannot be part of the approach to winning deals for Africans.

The Resource Power of Africa

African countries south of the Sahara have lots of resources; 30% of the world's known reserves of minerals (cobalt, diamonds, platinum, lithium, and uranium, etc.), 12 percent of oil reserves, 40 percent of gold deposits and 8% of gas resources. The continent has abundant renewable resources; land, forestry, water, and fishery. It has the second-largest tropical forest and roughly half of the world's most suitable land for farming. Natural resources make up over 70% of the continent's total exports and roughly 42% of national incomes across the board. Simply put, there is hardly any natural resource needed in this world that cannot be found in Africa. And the rest of the world needs it for manufacturing, industrial, energy, telecommunication, and other purposes. Without African resources, not much can be produced by the developed countries.

The question is, "How come a continent with such a scale of natural resources hosts the poorest of the poor in the world?" Many factors account for this situation; one of them being that African leaders are not winning deals for their people. For trade and bargaining power the rich natural resources are described by the international buyers as primary products, a nomenclature to place lower price tags on them.

It goes like this, an estate developer seeks to bargain for acres of land. In the process, he does a simulation for the landowner showing the splendid architectural work and drawings of high-rise buildings with gold-plated windows and shiny roofs. He builds a lively picture of how heaven-like the land will look on completion of the project. He applies the best of his negotiation skills to convince the landowner to give away his asset at a preferred price. The developer will not disclose to the landowner the estimated profits from the project. If the landowner fails to do due diligence on the current and estimated market value of the land and profitability of the project, and also does not appreciate that without his land the beautiful project will not materialize, he may end up being the loser.

Anybody who kick starts a deal with the mindset that his resources for bargaining are relatively trivial compared to those of the other party has already conditioned himself to receive less. Yes, he will become a loser because he failed to appreciate the incontrovertible fact that without his resources the other party cannot produce anything worth calling, "finished products." The buyer might look elsewhere. That is his option and not a matter of prime concern because all parties have options if only they take the trouble to look around and reason hard about the various offers.

One has to be proud of the worth of his resource, value it, and desist from making it look cheap. Otherwise, the other party takes advantage and comes back in the future with the same resource that he bought at a low price but cleverly transformed into several brands. He aims to make a fortune out of them, so he quotes each of the finished products at a high selling price. Once interest is expressed, then money will have to be spent. So the first seller (now reversed to be the buyer) uses the money he got from the initial transaction and may even have to look for additional resources to pay for the finished products of the seller who was previously the buyer of the raw material. So the astute dealmaker laughs all the way to the bank because he won the deal in the long run. For ages, this has been the end result of the raw materials from Africa.

The leaders should know the intrinsic value of their resources and be tough on that. Primarily, the deal making process requires adequate preparation. Dear reader, if you care for Africa, your head will spin if you see how leaders (politicians, bureaucrats, et cetera) prepare to enter into deals, particularly at the international level - a complete lack of preparation. The weaknesses are:

The Team: In many instances, African countries send teams whose members have inadequate expertise in the subject area. The criteria for selecting them sound funny at times. What happens sounds like this, "The matter relates to his Ministry/Department so, this and that person should go for the negotiation." Meanwhile, the selected people are clueless about how to cut a winnable deal. Will you send an amateur to a professional chess contest? No! Now compare this to the other party; who prepared diligently in advance having received relevant information about the African team. It mapped and established its choices for winning the deal ahead of time.

Timing: Hardly can anybody make a successful deal without factoring the "when" aspect into the itinerary. The time factor in negotiation is of immense importance especially, before and during the session. Do not rush into a negotiation when the scheduled date is short on notice because it does not facilitate adequate preparation. The same applies to the time of the meeting. Is it at a time that the physical body is refreshed or fatigued? Never go into a deal when your body is weak; physically, psychologically, emotionally, et cetera. Never concur to the time set by the other party without your input.

Venue: The venue for making deals counts a lot. It is like playing a football match on home ground as against playing away. The winning chances for the visiting team are slim. So it is with African governments when they engage international parties. Most often, they travel abroad to finalize the deal. The point is that there is a psychological game so when the host begins like this, "We are pleased to welcome you to our beautiful head office. I hope you had a wonderful trip. We have received your request for a facility of ... to be extended to you...," the visiting team should realize that there is in the statement an undertone to coax, and put it on the defense for "beggarly conduct." This is where toughness of character counts for the African deal maker - to gently accommodate, counter statements intelligently and at the same time, look diplomatically pretty.

Africans Can Win Deals

African leaders can win deals for Africans. What matters is for them to know the prioritized needs of their people and plan sufficiently for the negotiation. They need to do adequate analysis, asking themselves thus; "Do my people need this deal or can we do without it?" What are the specific things we need from the deal? What are their values and effects on livelihood? How high or low can we go so that by the end of the negotiation, we will still come away with an offer that is not less than what our country needs? For example, if it is a financial deal, how much minimum or maximum is a winnable deal? These points should be simulated in advance of the meeting.

Unfortunately, many African leaders have not demonstrated that they have adequate knowledge about their countries, people, and potential. The data for decision-making is defective and cannot make any meaningful impact on livelihood. The leaders are not proactive in analysis, scenario creation, and simulation to determine the impact of the credit facility they receive. In some instances, the loan/grant is seen as a windfall because it came unexpectedly when no determination was made of it in advance. Hence, it is misapplied or misused.

Let us ask ourselves, why does the lending party spread the interest on the loan over several years? It is because he calculated and knew the medium and long-term benefits. He does not crave a quick win in a deal. For example, Japan, South Korea, and Germany, after World War II, made a turnaround and are winners today of deals they made many years ago. But for Africa, it is a different story. The leaders strike quick-wins, hand-to-mouth deals, and Africans collectively find themselves in distress at the end. How long must this trend continue?

In his acceptance speech at the Republican Convention (2016),

['The Donald' gave a cue to making good deals thus, *"I pledge to never sign any trade agreement that hurts our workers, or that diminishes our freedom and independence. Instead, I will make individual deals with individual countries. No longer will we enter into these massive transactions, with many countries, that are thousands of pages long – and which no one from our country even reads or understands. We are going to enforce all trade violations against any country that cheats. This includes stopping China's outrageous theft of intellectual property, along with their illegal product dumping, and their devastating currency manipulation. Our horrible trade agreements with China, and many others, will be totally renegotiated. That includes renegotiating NAFTA to get a much better deal for America – and we'll walk away if we don't get the deal that we want."*]

So, to cut a good deal;

Know what you need: There are three primary takeaways in a deal (i) what you like to have or (ii) what you need to have, and (iii) what is available. The African deal maker can be assertive and dismiss baits when he knows what he needs. Losers fall to the snares of the deal (they settle on what they like or take what the other party says is available) thinking they have achieved something. No, they have not won the deal!

Have options: It should be remembered that there are options in deal-making. Just as the other party has options to look for another country that produces similar primary products, African leaders also have options to engage others who are prepared to transact business with them. It means leaders should have a database of such countries, institutions, corporate bodies, and individuals. They do not have to stick with a single dealer, no matter the bilateral or multi-lateral relationship over the years. One fine thing about open market is freedom of movement or choice which should be utilized to advantage. During the negotiation, there should be several options for the African team to maximize gains. The lack of options is one of the ways to fall prey to entrapments.

Passion for Winning: Deal making is a serious business. It has no room for lackadaisical proclivities. The African team should have a strong passion for success, commit itself strongly to the task and approach the negotiation with toughness, zeal and seriousness as if their whole life depends on winning a single deal.

After the deal is won: It is at this point that the real challenge for African leaders emerges. Will the resource be used to enhance the quality of life of Africans or the avarice of the leaders will set them against the fortunes of their people? Is it not a shame to see lending institutions sending their teams to monitor how Africans use the loans, grants, and other resources that have been given to them? It reflects weaknesses in moral character, discipline, and resource management.

The Planning Committee of the AU Arts Festival (2018) succinctly captures it thus "We can only achieve economic freedom and improve the livelihood of our people if resources earmarked for projects are put to use without any diversion."

One thing matters and needs to be said; when the resource is properly used, it reflects on the people, and they begin to trust their leaders. That is a rallying point for solidarity, working together, nation-building, and prayers for the country to keep winning big deals.

CHAPTER THREE

Defying the Odds

["It's time to deliver a victory for the American people. But to do that, we must break free from the petty politics of the past. America is a nation of believers, dreamers, and strivers that is being led by a group of censors, critics, and cynics. Remember: all of the people telling you that you can't have the country you want, are the same people telling you that I wouldn't be standing here tonight. No longer can we rely on those same people in the media, and politics, who will say anything to keep a rigged system in place. Instead, we must choose to Believe in America. History is watching us now. It's waiting to see if we will rise to the occasion, and if we will show the whole world that America is still free and independent and strong. I'm asking for your support tonight so that I can be your champion in the White House".]

Donald J. Trump, Acceptance Speech, GOP Convention, 2016

Often, it is said that African countries deserve the leaders they get because they (the leaders) are products of society. They are bred, shaped, and tolerated by societal beliefs, traditions, practices, and whatnots. So, in a critique of leadership performance, some people close the argument that society should bear a portion of the blame. This is a pathetic conclusion. If leaders only reflect the status quo, with time, that will lead to stagnation. If African leaders only mirror their societies, then any Tom, Dick and Harry could become a leader. But that cannot be the case; there should be something positively distinct and inspirational about a leader which genuine followers can strive to attain and lift up society. It is dangerous to have bootlickers whose motivation is not about the common good but to conspire and appropriate societal resources through dishonesty and shady deals.

It is however, a truism that a leader emerges from society but, on the assumption of office, he should progressively re-tool and drive society towards higher aspirations borne out of a realistic vision. The inauguration of that "something new" propels leaders beyond humdrum societal beliefs and practices. As much as possible, the leader does not make a radical change but sets new and higher standards and demonstrates them by a befitting lifestyle.

In realizing that dream, the leader should identify with the people he seeks to lead. It calls for sympathy and sharing of their past, aspirations, and values. He should understand their motivations, weaknesses, and strengths. When he understands his people enough, he can appreciate where the gaps exist and how bridged. It will be a disaster for him to think that he alone can bring about the needed change. He should guard against instilling hero worship in his followers which is bound to evaporate when the leadership position is lost because the people were not sufficiently prepared to own and live the vision beyond the physical presence of the leader.

There are many examples in Africa; from the immediate post-independence democratic period to military regimes. Some leaders made huge waves on coming into power but ebbed away to oblivion with time. Let us think about it. What accounts for the jubilation when civilian governments were overthrown? Again, why did the people celebrate when one military government after another was toppled? Why is today's democratic change of government occasioned by euphoria? The underlying factor is that the people did not internalize the ethos of the regimes.

The case of Ghana, the first independent country south of the Sahara, is worthy of reference. The early post-independent period saw rapid industrialization and infrastructural drive, which many scholars saw as valuable interventions. The pace of development was acclaimed to be equal to or above some of today's industrialized countries in Asia. Unfortunately, the country started experiencing a decline in living standards by 1966. So, when the democratic government was toppled in a military coup, the people went agog. What went wrong? Were the people so ignorant that they could not see the harm they were doing to themselves by celebrating military intervention? Was the leader so imbued with doing so many good things for his people that he left them behind?

That is how it plays out when there is a gap between the people and the leader's vision. The leader may even live the dream, but the people see only his heroic physical presence, not the vision he has brought forth. In such situations, charlatans see an opening to wade in and abort the governance process. It is a painful loss because the affected society will have to wait for some time and look for the reset button to move on again. After many years of agony and underdevelopment, the realization finally dawns on them, and they wondered why they allowed or participated in derailing their own development. They regretted the missed opportunity and longed for their past leader in abeyance of his vision. They tried to immortalize him by erecting giant and beautifully decorated edifices to remind themselves. But then, it is too late to bring back the past.

Since independence, it has been difficult for African leaders to share their vision with their people. They tried to effect changes through laws, policies, programs, and strategies with limited success. They could not defy the odds because to do so requires a collective effort, owned and fostered by the people. The leader's role is to identify what should change culturally, politically, and economically because they are hindrances to a free, quality, and happy life. The leader does not defy an idea, a belief or practice and leaves a vacuum. The axiom is "identity, defy and replace by adaptation." For this to happen, the leader should have an above-average experience in life, for which reason he can say, "I have seen it all" when confronted with a similar situation. It is critical and the reason it is said that leadership is not a child's play and charlatans should keep off.

Anybody who assumes a leadership position and tries to immediately, attack the existing establishment will likely run into trouble because the system for years, has taken tap root and integral to the office. As such, there should be a thorough situational analysis before any positive change. It takes time. But the ill-prepared leader who has not lived the situation in real life cares less if it works well or not. He thinks more of his personality, how to exalt himself and demonize others. As such, he becomes so detached from the results of his actions just like the worthlessness of the methods he used in the change process.

Any African leader who begins to defy the system he met in office without first defying the ills in his own life and character is a fraud. He is most likely to repeat the same mistakes or do worse or set others up and eventually, refuse to bear responsibility. The people who are serious in life are relentless, deep thinkers and astute at setting targets. They are practice-oriented and aggressive for getting results. They retrospect to identify their strengths, weaknesses, good works, and bad works. In their quiet times, they praised themselves where they did well and blamed themselves where they faltered to polish their observations, sense of judgment, and actions. They do not care much about external praise or condemnation but strive to learn their lessons every passing day. By identifying their personality flaws and working not to repeat such mistakes they learn to defy the tendency towards wrongful deeds. They sharpen their conscience to become increasingly responsive to every thought, word, and deed.

One may ask, what is the tool for this self-assessment? It is the same societal norms, values, traditions, and beliefs that are so complex in modern times because of externalities. The starting point is early childhood training in the home. The responsibility of parents to train their children properly deserves national attention because it is the basic unit where nation-building begins. It cannot be overstretched in this book.

'The Donald' said the following about his parents,

[*"My Dad, Fred Trump, was the smartest and hardest working man I ever knew. I wonder sometimes what he'd say if he were here to see this tonight. It's because of him that I learned, from my youngest age, to respect the dignity of work and the dignity of working people. He was a guy most comfortable in the company of bricklayers, carpenters, and electricians and I have a lot of that in me also. Then there's my mother, Mary. She was strong, but also warm and fair-minded. She was a truly great mother. She was also one of the most honest and charitable people I have ever known, and a great judge of character."]*

Thus, a leader goes through life, honing his character by experiencing the ups and downs. He keeps learning, and as he progressively increases his reach towards his ambition, he stocks enough capacity that naturally sets him apart from others. Through much agony and pain, he has become a gem. He does not see life on the surface but knows it is a serious enterprise within which there is a substance to lift up others. He is not motivated by appropriating material things in office but the singular virtue of making lives better for all without bias, favoritism, or ethnicity. The leader broadens his horizon to understand others and to increase his empathy. He would strive to be of greater service to his people, and depending on his level of truth (vision), he will endeavor to change any digressive status quo and attain not only for himself but for society. The ultimate is to win it for a better society. That is the leadership call in the true sense.

'The Donald' puts it thus,

[*"I have had a truly great life in business. But now, my sole and exclusive mission is to go to work for our country – to go to work for you. It's time to deliver a victory for the American people."*]

Truncation of Africa's Development

Numerous theses debate the developmental stage in African societies predating the arrival of visitors from Europe, the Mediterranean, and the Far East. Be it the Marxist theory of societal evolution and production, primitive communism, tribal-patriarchal societies, class societies, or feudalism, there is no denying that Africans were created like any other human beings, having their own socio-cultural, political, and economic systems of development, with unique internal mechanisms for renewal. There were empires, kingdoms, states, and even stateless societies whose occupation included agriculture, fishing, hunting, building, artisanship, trading, and means of production using appropriate technology.

The pioneering Ghana Empire (7th Century AD) was noted for its economic vivacity and traded with North Africa, East Africa, and the Middle East in salt, gold, and copper. It had a mixed economy of agriculture; goldsmith, iron smelting, pottery, carpentry, and cloth production.

Under Mansa Musa of Mali Empire (1312-1337 AD), Timbuktu became a prominent world cultural center. There were cases from the eastern, southern, and central parts of Africa in testimony that the continent was on the move and had reached an appreciable level of development before the arrival of unfamiliar persons from beyond. The level of progress might not be exactly that of Europe, the Americas, the Far East, and others. But homegrown systems held Africans together; in relative peace and unity; and enabled them to adopt new ways for improved and better living conditions.

Then the outsiders (from Europe) arrived with their baits (technology, machinery, means of production, and trade) that subdued a bourgeoning indigenous system across the continent. The introduction of the slave trade was a setback since it depleted labor and destroyed the existing means of local production. That is not to say that the phenomenon of slavery was not in Africa before the arrival of the visitors, but those slaves remained on the continent and were used to support the means of production. The externally-driven slave trade made it easier to subdue Africa, deepening colonialism and deprived the continent of many things in many ways.

Effects of Arrested Development

Nobody, especially the African, should underestimate the effects of colonialism on the continent because it was consequential; a reset button for Africa's development and contributed to the creation of a void that Africans have been struggling to fill. Primarily, it rendered the continent a producer of raw materials and a classic consumer of finished products that were manufactured from outside. It created an identity crisis, alienation, dependency syndrome, and the philosophical illusion that to succeed in life, an African has to be like a Westerner or live in the Western world. In other words, it mooted the fallacious belief that one must lose his African Identity to become successful.

The reader is referred to the following map which shows that only two African countries south of the Sahara (Sierra Leone and Ethiopia) were not colonized by Europeans. They were, however, affected by the spillovers of the perils of colonization.

Source: Edited by Grinker, R. R, Lubkemann S. C., Steiner C.B. (2010), Perspectives on Africa: A reader in culture, history and representation, Wiley- Blackwell (2nd Edition).

Political Colonization

One effect of the European advent is that Africa today has large clustered societies with characteristics such as; defined boundaries, established governance systems, adoption of an identifiable currency in the economy, conjoint practices, and the mode of assumption of political leadership generally defined and endorsed by the people. The defined territories may be called states or countries.

Previously, Africa was by distinct clusters of traditional territories and societies, but today they are fewer since many have come under one large single state. But to whose ultimate benefit? The Europeans did so to find an organizing principle for the continent since it was not possible for Africans to voluntarily merge their territories into single units except perhaps through conquest.

The partitioning of Africa at the Berlin Meeting in 1884/5 was to inaugurate something more than could immediately meet the eyes - to introduce a new European model for capturing political power on a foreign land. The intention was not to even introduce democracy but to peddle interest and coercive power to subdue African traditional leaders. They brought their governors to implant hybrid political arrangements and administer the territories. In the process, they established administrative and judicial systems, law and order regimes, and a system of formal education for Africans. By large, it was a requirement for every child in their territorial control to attend school. Meanwhile, the curriculum was European and had nothing to do with the African environment and technology. The emphasis was on proficiency in European languages to become a clerk or interpreter. The essentials to make the African industrious and entrepreneurial were left out.

Economically, there was a boom in trading activities in which European goods flooded the local markets. The colonialists introduced their currencies (monetization of African economies) as the official means of exchange, and Africans (who were not used to trading in currency) needed to work on the plantations and mines (which were taken over by the colonialists) to buy items or pay taxes. The colonialists kept a detailed register of tax-paying adults and severely punished those who defaulted.

Overall, an inversely proportional relationship developed between the traditional system and the colonial one; as the latter increased, the former kept reducing in power to the extent that social activities including marriage and naming ceremonies were gradually influenced. It is important to mention that the established political and administrative systems on the continent were not exclusive; they facilitated the European strategy to take over and dictate the economic direction of Africa.

Economic Colonization

The African continent was not an industrialized one prior to the arrival of Europeans. There were no large factories, use of heavy machinery, mass employment, and regular remuneration for workers. The economy was largely agrarian but in Europe, there was an upsurge of industrialization that required two things (i) a source of raw materials that were readily available in Africa, and (ii) additional markets since consumption was lower than production. It necessitated the search for new depots and markets to meet the demands of expansion and wealth creation.

The Berlin Meeting, therefore, decided that Africa should be "partitioned" among European countries. It authorized them to colonize and circumvent the existing traditional systems and modes of production on the continent. Thus, the European models got implanted, and by so doing, two things were achieved; i.e. to keep Africans as (i) producers of raw materials, and (ii) consumers of finished products from other parts of the world. The trading formula was to preserve the continent for the production of primary products including cotton, cocoa, coffee, groundnuts, palm oil, et cetera. The strategic objective was for Africans to produce what Europe needed but not what was appropriate for their local and national economies.

The colonialists controlled the market; they set limits on what goods should be exported and at what prices. Having the advantage of superior technology, they subjugated the indigenous ones and eventually rendered the people dependent on foreign goods. This situation inserted a psychological sensitivity in Africans that goods from foreign countries are better than those produced locally. Have the means of production and technology been developed, the continent would have been well-prepared to compete successfully on the global market. But no, this was not the case. One other significant point is that intra-continental trade which existed among Africans prior to the arrival of the Europeans was destroyed since the focus of the colonialists was to redirect trade between Europe and Africa.

By the 15th Century, imbalanced trade became a drag on Africa's development, and the economies of many countries became dependent on or controlled by external forces. The colonialists imposed various taxes to raise revenue and maintain law and order, which they needed for an uninterrupted supply of raw materials and trade. They would not spend on Africa; their home countries required the colonies to pay out of the modest income they raised from external trade.

There was a ridiculous agenda for infrastructure development; to develop only the sectors or areas that would facilitate production, transport, and export to Europe. There was absolutely, no desire, intention, or interest to improve the quality of life and living standards of Africans.

They administered the territories along the world view, culture, and practices of Europe. Ironically, they never had uniformity in their socio-cultural and political arrangements. And since they had diverse systems and approaches to colonization, it further deepened the division among Africans. For instance, the British adopted indirect rule because they were more interested in exploiting resources. They did not interfere in the socio-cultural practices of their colonies, unlike the French whose philosophy was to indoctrinate their colonies (Policy of Assimilation) which led to the adoption of direct rule. For the Europeans to effectively prosecute their strategic objective, they integrated some Africans into the established political and administrative systems.

Indoctrinated African Elites and Identity Crisis

Political independence across the continent gave birth to a class of political "hermaphrodites" who could be dubbed "African-by-Nature and European-by-Nurture." They were the ones who received formal education and had the privilege of working in colonial offices. They saw formal education as a means to get rich and enjoy a better life. They hardly saw it as a means of enlightenment to support or lift up their fellow Africans. Their ego was to dominate others in the absence of the colonialists.

There was yet another class who were semi-literate but trained professionally to keep law and order. The underlying objective was to protect the colonial masters' life and property. Together, the two classes became the instruments for breaking the African stance, to conquer territories, seize lands and mines, appropriate for pleasure, put fear into the people and subdue them. They treaded the footsteps of the Europeans and became part of the European politico-administrative system, and without any holdback, acted for and with them rather than in the interest of their fellow Africans.

The situation had a swelling effect on them since it triggered an identity crisis. The European, from birth, belongs to a comprehensive society (State) without any smaller units (called traditional societies) to fall on. The point here is that, unlike Africans, the Europeans had formed their States (bottom-up) before they came to Africa and by the Berlin Declaration (using maps without any care about separation of families) grouped Africans into comprehensive societies (top-down) to serve their interest.

The colonialists were not totally successful in their attempt to recondition Africans because a majority remained guided by tradition, but those who worked for them, the "African-by-Nature and European by-Nurture" shillyshallied between tradition and the requirements of the alien comprehensive society (State). They developed personality conflict about authority, control, allegiance, world view of life, thought processes, culture, aspirations, and practices. With time they stepped into the positions that were once occupied by the colonialists and took over the assets, governance, and development deficits left by them. Make no mistakes, "independence" did not eliminate the political, economic, and social systems built or impacted by the Europeans; they remain to date as instruments of action in the hands of the personality conflicted leaders to govern the people.

The whole struggle for independence is like a situation where a group of people on a journey complained that the driver (who happened to be European) was not smart on the steering wheel. The mechanic (African trained by the European) saw an opportunity, and together with the passengers, got rid of the driver. Meanwhile, the bus was programmed to travel at 40km/hour compared to the 240km/hour required to arrive on time. What would the change of driver do to get the passengers there early? Nothing! The identification by color, origin, language, and personality traits with the apprentice is immaterial in this matter because the vehicle would still not respond to time.

The solution is to fix it, and, in case the passengers choose to do so, the mechanic is well-placed to play a role depending on his technical knowledge, skills and orientation. Imagine that he was unskilled, or wants to make a fortune out of the situation by dishonesty then, the situation of the travelers would get worse. Such is the African story; the matter goes beyond political independence and now rests with today's African leaders.

The Western Politico-Administrative System

Europe was once in the condition of Africa by the 5th century. There was nothing like autonomous states as we have them by the names of United Kingdom, Spain, France, Portugal, Denmark, et cetera. Rather, there were empires; the last ones being the Roman Empire, and the Frankish Empire. Even as they existed, other organized peoples from nearby territories frequently fought against them. The empires were purposively organized entities with features that included;

    i.   a political system;

    ii.   common laws that were enforceable;

    iii.   allegiance to the emperor;

    iv.   a tax determination and collection system;

    v.   infrastructure provision to support livelihood, trade and movement of goods and people;

    vi.   progressive proliferation of cultural values and practices;

    vii.   a built-up economy and system for the exchange of goods and services, and

    viii.   educational system to promote learning.

These characteristics were the means by which societies met their needs in an organized manner. They were not exclusive to Europe, but could be found in Africa even before the arrival of the colonialists.

There was something peculiar about religion. It was required of the vassals to worship the god of the empire, but when it went against the mode of worship or belief system of the vassals, there was always resistance. The opposition was often interpreted as bad citizenship and the call for the Emperor to enforce the laws by taking punitive measures. But the educational system (emphasizing science, art, and attitudes) enabled the vassals to think beyond their immediate group and act as recognized members of the empire; one people with a common practice and aspiration.

History shows that the region which is now Europe after the fall of the Roman Empire was a volatile area inundated by conflict, revolt, and wars. The then existing political, economic, and social systems highlighted wealth, ownership of slaves and land as the basis for power, control, and social recognition. Unlike Africa, where land was community owned and held in trust by the traditional authority, feudalism was the stock-in-trade in Europe. The landowners bought people to work on their lands, who could only work harder to regain their freedom. The laws were harsh and initially upheld the practice, but as time went by they were reviewed. The lords of the lands swore allegiance to the emperor and often committed resources on negotiated terms. The arrangement did not permit any lord to put his peasants/common people under the direct control of the emperor. It was a faulty political line so during the period of spontaneous revolts by the peasants the emperor could not give any military support.

Again, history shows that feudalism wrecked anarchy in Europe. The civil government and the papacy, regardless of isolated differences worked together. They even proclaimed themselves, in the midst of inhuman practices as representatives of God, to the disdain of the people and an eventual push towards equality of rights. The socio-political system promoted assumption of high office by means of (i) religious backing (ii) aristocracy (iii) feudal control. The effect was that it bolstered powerful forces to fight among themselves for supremacy all the time. In the process, the peasants became instruments for war, life, and death.

The catastrophic European experience was not part of African history. The traditional laws kept religion separate from the political system and made provisions for how a leader or chief could be enstooled or destooled. For example, the failure of a leader to treat his people deservedly is enough justification for destoolment. No traditional leader ever had absolute power or came close to being seen as a representative of God. The historical records show that the

European love for materiality was the cause of upheavals, wars, and bloodshed wherever they go; whether in Europe, India, America, or Africa. They fought among themselves, and other people on earth whom they inaccurately claimed they discovered.

In their home countries, at the opportune time, the inhumane and oppressive old order was aggressively overthrown by the masses during the period termed the "Reign of Terror." In France, for example, both rich and poor, lord and peasant, clergy and the common, after shedding so much blood, eventually resolved that they needed to part ways with the terrible economic, political, and social order and replace it with a unique one, founded on the overarching principle of equality of rights. By so doing, the Europeans ended the abuse of power, non-accountability for the use of resources, arbitrary decision, subjugation of the masses by the few, human rights abuses, despotic laws, papacy connivance, cronyism, favoritism, and above all, the discredited philosophy behind the distinction and differential practices between the nobles and the masses.

The Declaration of Rights of Men in France (Robinson, J.H. 1908) for instance, stated as follows,

["*Men are born and remain equal in rights. Social distinctions can only be founded upon the general good." "Law is the expression of the general will. Every citizen has a right to participate, personally or through his representative, in its formation. It must be the same for all." "No person shall be accused, arrested, or imprisoned except in the cases and according to the forms prescribed by law." "No one shall be disquieted on account of his opinions, including his religious views, provided that their manifestation does not disturb the public order established by law." "The free communication of ideas and opinions is one of the most precious of the rights of man. Every citizen may, accordingly, speak, write, and print with freedom, being responsible, however, for such abuses of this freedom as shall be defined by law." "All citizens have a right to decide, either personally or by their representative, as to the necessity of the public contribution, to grant this freely, to know to what uses it is put, and to fix the proportion, the mode of assessment and of collection, and the duration of the taxes." "Society has the right to require of every public agent an account of his administration." Well might the Assembly claim, in its address to the people, that "the rights of man had been misconceived and insulted for centuries," and boast that they were "reëstablished for all humanity in this declaration, which shall serve as an everlasting war cry against oppressors."]*

The administrative arrangement was the means to operationalize the political system. It was established in every territory and focused on taxation, security, laws, records management, sanctions, infrastructure, health, and education. It was vibrant, changing according to the dynamics of the political system. It was improved to ably protect the people against the vagaries of any politician or administrator whose political or personal conduct was against the laid down laws, practices, and values. The law prescribed sanctions, and it was a requirement for the administrative branch, in particular, to carry them out to the letter without regard to person.

It should be mentioned that despite the ills of feudalism and the subsequent class system that it created, people worked to produce for their lords, and as commerce, especially with the Orient increased, there came a time that it became necessary to manufacture for surplus. Trade with the East (this strange European taste for spices in those days) was a driving factor in the sea travels and the rise of Portuguese maritime power. From Christopher Columbus to Vasco da Gama and Magellan, commerce was a trigger to set sail but not to supplant political systems in other lands. Being favored with emerging knowledge about the world including astronomy, medicine, and the revolt against the Roman Catholic Church by Protestants, Europe was ready to ascend higher rungs of social and political order and inaugurate new thoughts and practices. There was a proliferation in culture, learning, philosophy, arts, science, and technology. Great inventions were made; gunpowder, steam, railways, and printing which facilitated the establishment of factories and increased productivity beyond the immediate consumption of the people. To dispose of the excess, Europe needed to find new buyers.

The lesson from the preceding points is that the political system in Europe was built on who the people are, their historical past and the lessons learned, their culture, beliefs, and general worldview of life. It also included and more importantly, their economic aspirations and how they (Europeans) envisioned their society to be, not only for today but in the future. It prioritized the nuclear family and a sense of individual responsibility and rights.

The training of the individual involves the acquisition of knowledge of the law and the State structure. He is taught to owe allegiance (including civic responsibility) to the State and the institutions of the State and, also, demand what is due him because it is a right. The political system was initiatory for progress, pillared on values, principles, and standards that all are to observe. It was not a perfect system, but progressively Europeans continue to refine it.

How could such a politico-administrative system be implanted in another territory like Africa (which has never gone through similar turbulent periods in its history), and it would be expected to function conveniently for Africans? If it did, it was to the advantage of the privileged few who adapted themselves to the European mode. These were the people who more or less took over the remnants of state architecture (which was bequeathed by the colonial masters) and sought to perfect them amid the worldviews of Africans against the European establishment.

Legitimacy: The African, deep down in his heart, doubted the legitimacy of the state government for usurping the authority of traditional leaders. The Western-styled laws were alien to him, and at times conflicted with traditional ones. Their application was even more problematic. For example, sanctions under foreign laws were carried out in ways that were not only strange but exuded fear and disbelief among the indigenes. This is because sanctions in African tradition were tailored more at reformation (for the offender to realign with society) than a punitive measure.

The local people saw in the slavery days many of their brothers and sisters, husbands and wives, and the able-bodied, who provided the family's needs, rounded up and forcibly taken away into slave castles. They saw others openly shot and killed like a game for trying to escape. They knew that power was to be exercised to protect the people and promote their well-being but not the other way around. Consequently, they could not bring themselves up to accept European domination, much more when their traditional leaders were still around and defending them against colonial abuse.

The issue of trust: The entry strategy of the colonialists did not endear them to Africans. They cajoled, coerced, seized, killed, and bought their way through to possess the lands, mines, and forests. They commercialized the lands for cash crops while the local people went hungry, and introduced forced labor, which was patterned along feudalism whereby those who worked had to endure strict rules and work harder in exchange for their freedom if they ever had it. They forced the African indigenes to work on the plantations and mines and paid them low wages.

The European politico-administrative system made an impression on the people to the effect that it was a gate-way to wealth, the hen that lays the golden egg for a happy life, a place where the resources from the local system are kept and should be plundered rather than for investment and societal development. This characterization became compounded as a result of poor capacity-building programs that would enable Africans to have strategic minds for effective organization and management of state affairs. Their training was to make them clerks, pushing files from one office to the other, and also, for them to serve as interpreters, who were fit for junior positions. The African was left out of the strategic policy decision-making process.

Perception of government: The colonialists operated a centralized state system with a lot of power in the hands of the governor as the chief representative of his home country. The government was not based on democratic tenets because the colonial interest was not to develop democracy in Africa. The alignment of government and administrative systems was to facilitate the exploitation of African resources. The decisions taken were without any consultation or participation of the local people. Similarly, there were no public educational programs to increase the people's awareness about their roles, rights, and responsibilities. In effect, the Africans became unconnected to the State and government.

Ethnicity: The colonial masters exploited the presence of varied ethnic groups across the continent. They did not promote unity among them because they did not want the people to mobilize themselves and rise up against them. Accordingly, balance and equity in service and infrastructural provision became bargaining chips to win allegiance and favor friendly ethnic groups.

In the face of these colonial proclivities, the Africans grew to detest the bequeathed European establishment, seen as an oppressive instrument that should be opposed as much as possible, and in case something good was found, it should be appropriated in conciliation.

Take-Aways from Colonialism

Even though the European intervention was a derailment of Africa's homegrown development, it had some positive effects. Firstly, it led to the creation of large societies (states) that became the foundation for organizing people in a defined jurisdiction along socio-economic, political, and administrative lines. Perhaps, Africans eventually, would have done that by themselves but it would likely take a longer time with attendant upheavals. Secondly, the introduction of formal education was a push to raise the psycho-motor-affective aspects of Africans. It is a critical resource for any meaningful socio-economic development. Western education facilitated the emergence of the class of African elites, among whom dedicated ones fought for independence on the continent.

Thirdly, a system for economic organization was introduced (based on competitive resource areas) for international trade including cotton, cocoa, coffee, tea, diamonds, gold, et cetera. Africa had an entry point to world trade, and the opportunity exists to add value to its products towards comparative advantage. In addition, the rudimentary roadmap that prioritized natural resources for economic and infrastructural development was established.

Finally, learning foreign languages (for example, English and French) enabled Africans to become part of the universal integration efforts. It created the opportunity for people to associate and build friendships all over Europe and the world. This is not to say that it could not have happened without colonization, but it would have taken a longer time and not at a faster rate than it has been achieved.

Overall, colonialization provided the initial political and socio-economic framework for development across African countries. It means when the framework is re-aligned and implemented, the living standards of the people on the continent could improve beyond what it is today. It, however, depends on how well African leaders are prepared to remake their countries against the odds.

The African Odds

What did African leaders inherit at independence? To answer this question, a summary of the situation at independence is presented in Table 1. It compares interventions in specific political, social, economic and technological areas betweem Africans and Europeans and the ultimate effects on former.

Table 1: Profile of Africa at Independence

Thematic Area	African Intervention	European Intervention	Effect on Africans
Resources	Internal use	Seized and exported	Depleted
Labor	Used in agrarian economy	Forced and used for cash crops and mining	Exploited
Taxation	Non-existence	Rigidly implemented	Biased, Unfavorable
Industrialization	Non-existence	Not introduced	Unchanged
Economy	Agrarian	Cash crops, monetized	Low food production
Trade	Internal	Exports to Europe	Biased, Unfavorable
Traditions, culture, values	Promote social cohesion	Denigrate, change to European system	Fragmented
Psyche	Linked to African tradition	Indoctrinate, linked to European system	Inferiority complex
Political	Traditional rulership	Set boundaries, create new systems and administration, no elections, indirect/ direct external rule	Undermined traditional political system
Education	Not formalized	Formalized, imposed, based on European system	Nurtured to be like Westerner but having no skills.
Technology	Formative	Heavy machinery	African

	stage		technology abandoned.
Modes of Production	Formative but linked to environment	Advanced but linked to European environment	Aborted/ Terminated
Wages	Not emphasized	Monetized labor, introduced European currencies, paid low.	Exploited
Infrastructure	Not emphasized or communal	Biased, European style, built around exploited resource areas.	Very limited coverage
Medicine	Traditional	Indoctrinate	Changed to Western.
Religion	Traditional	Indoctrinate	Changed to Western.
Language	Develop as per indigene	Develop European ones.	Dual (local and European) observed
Marriage	Traditional	Along European procedure	Dual (local and European) observed.
Conflict Management	Traditional arbitration	Along European procedure	Less attention on traditional system.
Identity	Communal	Individualistic	Personality conflict
Sense of responsibility	Communal	Individualistic	Displaced onto a

			second party.
Ownership of land	Communal	Individualistic	Conflict in family ownership.

Author's construct: February, 2024

In addition, the question remains about how a besmirched traditional system could run side-by-side with the European system. More importantly, could African leaders be selfless and morally courageous to avoid the enticements of the positions they have come to occupy?

Living Standards in Africa

Is the government of Africa delivering on the essence of independence, to lift up people, make them earn a decent livelihood and unearth their God-given talents? How come that over 50 years since independence, the specter of abject poverty is rife and fast spreading across the continent?

Year by year, world development reports and indexes consistently rate many African countries below acceptable living standards. The reports of the International Monitoring Fund, World Bank, United Nations, and even in-house statistics of African countries point to the reality of poorness. Take, for instance, the Human Development Index of the United Nations over the past ten years, and the likely conclusion is that most African countries fall in the category of average to low human development.

If one should single out poverty or income (or non-income) levels, the result is more startling because sub-Saharan Africa, compared to other parts of the world, ranks as one of the poorest regions. That implies that literacy, life expectancy, and well-being are low. It is hard to believe that people are dying from preventable diseases such as cholera and malaria because of inadequate access to clean water and sanitation. Infant and maternal mortality rates are on the increase and there is a prevalence of poor dietary intake and weight loss, particularly among children of school-going age despite the vast tracts of fertile land on the continent.

It is unfathomable that Africa, having so much of the Earth's uncultivated lands, suffers to get results-driven leaders (across governance and institutional spheres) to achieve food self-sufficiency. The continent is a net importer of food from other parts of the world, spending roughly US$36 billion yearly, and estimated to be a whooping US$110 billion by 2025. Is it not sad that the agricultural sector has over 60% concentration of Africa's labor force yet there is a shortage of nutritious food? The highest importers of rice in the world in 2017 were from Sub-Saharan Africa. As reported by CNN on 4/02/17, out of the top 25 rice-importing countries, Africa alone had nine countries.

For renewable water use, Africans are at an estimated value of two which is below the world average standard of five. Out of roughly 783 million people who do not have access to safe drinking water, Sub-Saharan Africa alone has close to 319 million people. Over 102 million people from an estimated number of 159 million still rely on untreated surface water for drinking, cooking, bathing, and washing. The lack of access to safe and clean water coupled with poor sanitation, is a major contributor to the increasing incidence of water-borne diseases in the region. Life expectancy, for instance, is declining and hovers around 45-55 years compared to Asian countries that are rising and in the range of 65-75 years.

The water bodies and the environment are under destruction from mining, logging, and other economic activities to the extent that there is an upsurge in health hazards and climate change conditions. In all this, it is not only the horrific statistics of poor living standards across Africa today that should be of concern but also, the trajectory of a worse condition in the future that should be most troubling and demands a fierce urgency of action.

Politico-Administrative Model in Africa

It is a fact that the formal politico-administrative system in Africa at national and local levels imitates the western one. One may wonder why this situation. Was it an attempt to make an easy choice by the formally educated "African-by-Nature and European-by-Nurture?" Is it that there was no original thinking to develop a unique governance system that reflects African Identity?

It is incontrovertible that the authentic governance system in the land, time-tested and still connects and holds the people together is the traditional system. It holds sway even in complex urban areas even during the colonial days. It still clutches the lands in trust for the people, promotes local development, builds unity, ensures the safety of self and property, and encourages participation and civic responsibility. It lives on despite attempts by many African governments to dismantle or undermine or ignore it especially during the early post-independence periods.

Is it not baffling that scholars fail to see that the western system, (as fine as it may be) is somehow appreciated by the literate "African-by-Nature and European-by-Nurture" relative to the majority of Africans? Is it not a wonder how leaders who are adept at imitating European systems could be so inept at formulating a unique African governance system? Either they have a weak strategic mind or are adverse to strengthening or accommodating the traditional governance system or are simply intolerant of any other complementary source of state authority.

Western Model

So, the Europeans built an administrative set-up to secure their political system by defining and directing the relationship that should exist among all stakeholders. Its cardinal qualities include equity, fairness, responsibility, transparency, and accountability in the management of the collective resources of the State. Based on their history, they preferred the independence of institutions in the execution of their functions without any influence from any entity.

The administrative structures and processes were designed to guide the office and those who work in and out of it. The education, training, and exposure were to adequately prepare the individual from his youthful stages (in thoughts, words, and actions) to relate to his environment and to defend the State and its institutions that offer him protection and security in life.

The mode of employment was strictly by the merit system without any underhand dealings. The administrative process is based on competition and thrives on people with excellence. There are career and personal development programs, clear-cut rules and regulations, and sanctions are applied without favor when breached. The value system stemmed from their past struggles and the workers are obliged to see everyone as having equal rights. The relationship between the public administration system, the private sector and civic society is symbiotic to drive development across board into the future. The added advantage of public service is that it comes with societal recognition, self-worth, and honor for sincere and hardworking officeholders. The Europeans uphold it as the mechanism to protect State cohesion and therefore, frowns upon its abuse.

Unfortunately, those qualities are yet to constitute an integral part of the African politico-administrative system. There are hardly any productive periodic reviews aimed at modernizing it in response to the dynamics of the times. Many political leaders adduced reasons to explain away why institutional renewal should not be done, and most often, the attribution is to the lack of funds. Meanwhile, there is unbridled desire to expend on protocols, travels and transport, parties, ceremonies, and whatnot. Unfortunately, the literate "African-by-Nature and European-by-Nurture" sees the public administration system as a tool to serve his interest and would hardly make it function independently of himself. The administrative laws, policies and standards mean little to him so, and for whatever reason, the sector is generally kept in the same old-fashioned manner with superficial reforms. The structure, process, resource, and personnel are designed and continue to be dominated by a free-riding political class, and coupled with an absence of enforcement/security/protection for the public officer, the public sector is gradually losing its potency to effectively work for the general good of the people in Africa.

The Defiance

Essence of governance: It is said that any governance system that is not built on the tradition, culture, values, aspirations, and economy of the people will suffer difficulties and imminent failure. The successful adventure of Europeans to Africa provides a useful lesson that the *raison d'etre* for constructing a political system is to meet the necessities of life of people but not for private gain. The political system should yield certain tangible results such as; food, shelter, education, health, security, civic responsibility, freedoms and rights, effective mobilization and resource use, transparency and accountability, and overall improved standards of living.

The African situation seems hopeless and many people have given up on the continent. In this day and age, many Africans (especially the youth) are pre- disposed to the notion that the promise of a better life on earth is elsewhere but not in Africa. Hardly does a month pass by without news of boat tragedies in which Africans got drowned in the Mediterranean Sea. This is aside the dangerous stowaways, hijacks and other illegal attempts to run away. Visit the embassies, high commissions, and consulates and you would hardly believe what met your eyes; the long meandering queues, the struggles, and the anxieties expressly written on the faces of people as they tried to acquire visas to Europe, Asia, Americas, and of late, Middle East. A friend once cracked a joke that, "unlike the old slavery days when Europeans came looking for slaves, today it is the African in search for a slave master."

By what conditioning has it become a part of the African psyche that quality life prevails elsewhere but not in Africa? Certainly, this position is not part of the values underlying the independence struggle. Therefore, collective leadership action is required across all African countries to arrest the situation. It means the governance process must yield livelihood results, and the leader should mean what he says and says what he means. He should show the way, not only in words but in character and deeds.

Firstly, he should have a clear and realistic vision out of a cumulative understanding of the African situation. He should share his vision and the expected changed state with the people to create ownership. We see a classic example in "Animal Farm" - that enthralling book written by George Orwell in 1946 - where at an evening meeting, Old Major communicated his dream to the other animals about rebellion against their human masters and the subsequent declaration of independence.

It was a moving speech in which he described the current horrible conditions of the animals and their eventual terrible end if they failed to take action. He painted a vivid picture of the beautiful future awaiting them if they drove out human beings from the farm.

A similar example is found in the Bible about the Israelites and their movement from captivity to freedom. Exodus 3:7-8 says,

[*"And the Lord said, I have surely seen the affliction of my people which are in Egypt, and have heard their cry by reason of their taskmasters; for I know their sorrows; and I am come down to deliver them out of the hand of the Egyptians, and to bring them up out of that land unto a good land and a large, unto a land flowing with milk and honey; unto the place of the Canaanites, and the Hittites, and the Amorites, and the Perizzites, and the Hivites, and the Jebusites."*]

'The Donald' did a similar thing. His slogan, "Make America Great Again" alone tells the expected future state. His acceptance speech at the Republican Convention (2016) gave some indications;

[*"Together, we will lead our party back to the White House, and we will lead our country back to safety, prosperity, and peace. We will be a country of generosity and warmth. But we will also be a country of law and order. Our Convention occurs at a moment of crisis for our nation. The attacks on our police, and the terrorism in our cities, threaten our very way of life. Any politician who does not grasp this danger is not fit to lead our country. Americans watching this address tonight have seen the recent images of violence in our streets and the chaos in our communities. Many have witnessed this violence personally, some have even been its victims. I have a message for all of you: the crime and violence that today afflicts our nation will soon come to an end. Beginning on January 20th 2017, safety will be restored. The most basic duty of government is to defend the lives of its own citizens. Any government that fails to do so is a government unworthy to lead."*]

[*"Again, I will tell you the plain facts that have been edited out of your nightly news and your morning newspaper: Nearly Four in 10 African - American children are living in poverty, while 58% of African-American youth are not employed. 2 million more Latinos are in poverty today than when President Obama took his oath of office less than eight years ago. Another 14 million people have left the workforce entirely. Household incomes are down more than 4 thousand dollars since the year 2000 – 16 years ago. Our trade deficit in goods reached nearly 800 billion dollars last year alone. The budget is no better. President Obama has almost doubled our national debt to more than 19 trillion dollars, and growing. Yet, what do we have to show for it? Our roads and bridges are falling apart, our airports are in Third World condition, and forty-three million Americans are on food stamp."*]

On the American economy, he said,

["*I will outline reforms to add millions of new jobs and trillions in new wealth that can be used to rebuild America*" ..."*My message is that things have to change – and they have to change right now. Every day I wake up determined to deliver a better life for the people all across this nation that have been ignored, neglected and abandoned. I have visited the laid-off factory workers, and the communities crushed by our horrible and unfair trade deals. These are the forgotten men and women of our country. People who work hard but no longer have a voice. I AM YOUR VOICE. I have embraced crying mothers who have lost their children because our politicians put their personal agendas before the national good. I have no patience for injustice, no tolerance for government incompetence, no sympathy for leaders who fail their citizens. When innocent people suffer, because our political system lacks the will, or the courage, or the basic decency to enforce our laws – or worse still, has sold out to some corporate lobbyist for cash – I am not able to look the other way.*"]

He depicted the expected future state in these words,

["*With these new economic policies, trillions of dollars will start flowing into our country. This new wealth will improve the quality of life for all Americans. We will build the roads, highways, bridges, tunnels, airports, and the railways of tomorrow. This, in turn, will create millions more jobs.*"]

In conclusion he said thus,

["*My pledge reads: "I'M WITH YOU – THE AMERICAN PEOPLE." I am your voice. So to every parent who dreams for their child, and every child who dreams for their future, I say these words to you tonight: I'm with you, I will fight for you, and I will win for you. To all Americans tonight, in all of our cities and in all of our towns, I make this promise: We Will Make America Strong Again. We Will Make America Proud Again. We Will Make America Safe Again. And We Will Make America Great Again. God bless You and Good Night.*"]

Many examples abound all over the globe including those of past African leaders. But as mentioned earlier, having a dream is only the beginning of a tortuous journey. There are hurdles, one major one being how to create ownership for the vision. It calls for developing dynamic strategies and building the team for mentoring - a factor that is badly missing in the leadership trajectory of Africa. Not that type of mentoring built on dynasty. Examples in Togo, Gabon, Equatorial Guinea, and Congo D.R. reflect "dynasty in democracy" which is not the path Africa should choose at the national level since many leaders lack a thorough understanding of the purpose of life and the African situation.

Institution Building for the Vision

Building the structure and designing an appropriate and enduring process to actualize the vision is challenging. It requires critical thinking and taking the precise measures. Beyond institutional structure and process, the leader and his team should live by "collective decision." That is to say, the leader should be doing it right and be seen by the people as such. In addition, he should have a monitoring and evaluation system (backed by rigorous statistics) for evidence-based results on the quality of life of the people. The fluid conditions of modernity (which will be more intense in the future) require dynamism but not process regimentation in living the vision.

The defiance of the status quo should seek to transform the lurching negativities of Africa into positivity. The leaders should consider the following guideposts;

1. cut out the inward-looking materialistic tendency - that is not the purpose of life and leadership. When it comes to the crunch, leaders are not made by material possessions but how they lift up people for improved quality of life;

2. change the African "it cannot be done" mentality and the inferiority complex. Replace with the "can-do" spirit and adequate levels of exposure, particularly during youthful years;

3. identify and remove corruption foisting inclinations from the scheme of things, especially hero worship.
4. transform retrogressive value systems;
5. develop a new African brand by moving away from the old ways that got Africa negatively tagged;
6. reduce or eliminate the politics of exclusiveness and "winner-takes- all";
7. snip off appointment by favoritism, ethnicity, familiarity, and association;
8. divest from external to internally generated resource use, and
9. develop and utilize an African transformation agenda to create wealth and improve the quality of life for the people.

There are many more decisive actions that a leader could take depending on the present and future conditions. One certainty is that the more frequent questions like - "Is it working for the people? Is it making their lives better?" - are asked, the stronger the leader connects with reality. Reliance on oral feedback alone from subordinates does not make a good leader in Africa. Field visits (sometimes unannounced) give first-hand knowledge on governance effectuality.

CHAPTER FOUR

Spoils of Multi-Party Democracy

["No one pretends that democracy is perfect or all-wise. Indeed, it has been said that democracy is the worst form of government except all those other forms that have been tried from time to time."]

Sir Winston Churchill (1874-1965), former Prime Minister of Britain

There is no human institution that is so impeccable that no defects can be found with it and vice versa. Even for a sophisticated governance system like democracy (considered here as free and the direct or indirect application of authority originating from the people), it cannot be the case that it is without blemish.

If an individual masters how to defy the odds to realize his higher-performing self, it becomes easier, in many instances to feed on the spoils of multi-party democracy. The democracy in vogue is not really new to the world. History shows that it has always been part of human evolution in degrees, but aspects differ depending on the intricacies of societies.

Its defects have little to do with the lofty philosophy, values, and precepts it propounds. Often, the problem is with the people who practice it but even there they can be excused for their inadequacies because the democratic tenets propounded by the founding fathers in the West were in different eras. Take the United States of America for example; the flight from Europe and consequent founding of the new land, the struggles against colonial rule, and the Declaration of Independence in 1776 occurred for a certain class of people whose history, experiences, and aspirations bound them together, and triggered their resolution to form a Union, and to be guided by a Constitution whose cardinal points are to (i) resist any subjugation by a fellow human being or religious belief system (ii) form and oblige governments not to interfere in people's lives, but to carry out their wish and guarantee a happy life for them in the spirit of equality and in the supreme recognition that everyone was uniquely endowed by the Creator.

The political foundation was laid over 200 years ago, and at that time it would not have made much sense to prevail upon the founding fathers to welcome what we call today globalization and free trade. Neither would it be acceptable to tell them to call some people "immigrants" and to cut them out for that matter. The USA was built on a succor identity to (i) be the hope for the hopeless and inspiration for those who felt let down and (ii) demonstrate that it stands for all humanity. That was then; today, world conditions trend differently and require a different political energy.

The USA does not need to think about neo-colonialization in any form or shape or the denial of rights and freedoms to its people. After two centuries of independence, these values have become ingrained into the social order. Similarly, she has steadfastly become the most powerful country the world has ever known in modern history. But internally, there was a general disagreement among the people about the way forward towards the desired state of a happy life. The division was inherently deep and threatened the fundamentals that built the political system. For some people, the Constitutional demand on governments that Americans live a happy life did not reflect in their lives. The conditions as identified by 'The Donald' included;

    i.   illegal immigration and the concomitant unlawful traffic of drugs, cash, guns, and people across the borders. The effect was harmful to Americans; financially, the cost was close to 113 billion dollars a year;

   ii.   unfair relationship with other countries to the detriment of the USA;

  iii.   internal insecurity that has led to the loss of many innocent lives;

  iv.   loss of jobs because of companies moving to other countries;

   v.   politicians reaping from the perks of government while the masses

of people suffered;

i.   the raging poverty, especially in the inner cities;
ii. dysfunctional factories;
iii. ineffective educational system; and
iv. increasing crime and drug trafficking.

These issues are about livelihood and human dignity and, if democracy is the standard bearer for every development (sine quo nom), those negative conditions would not have prevailed in the USA to the point that the people would vote for a change. 'The Donald's message resonated with the masses just as it was in Europe at the dawn of a new era of freedom, equality, equity, and the rule of the Commons. At his inaugural address, he made poignant referrals that touched the hearts and minds of the masses;

[*"We are one nation and their pain is our pain. Their dreams are our dreams. And their success will be our success. We share one heart, one home, and one glorious destiny. The oath of office I take today is an oath of allegiance to all Americans."*]

Democracy assures the masses of political rights and all manner of freedoms. It pivots on their sovereignty and participation but does not necessarily secure the necessities of life for them. It hinges on issues of rights and freedoms (of life, property, speech, association and religion), separation of state powers, and separation of state from religion. Unfortunately, the standards do not necessarily lead to economic breakthroughs for the masses. Functionally, it affords the people the opportunity to elect a leader in a divided multi-party manner that eventually creates the situation of a winner and loser among them. But in a good spirit, the victor and the vanquished should learn to work together. It is a hard thing to do, except there exists a high level of civility, tolerance, and discipline.

The rule of majority has inherent danger in the face of weak or disregard for state institutions. There are several cases the world over where acclaimed democracies deteriorated, and out of the chaos, a new system of governance evolved. Machiavelli, in the theory of cyclical government, points to this sorry state of democracy; he did not see the rule of the majority as a political arrangement fait accompli. Rather, the majority may become inward-looking, overly confident, and delivering governance functions without much consideration for the development effect on other people. This situation, if it continues to trend, will lead to revolt and eventual anarchy from which a hero will emerge and begin the rule of one person. When the person is not checked by any existing parallel institution, it will result in tyranny and the consequent emergence of a monarchy. The theory does not see any permanency of one particular political system. It allures to the bounded linkages of periodic decline and re-emergence of monarchy, aristocracy, and democracy types of political arrangements.

Much of the post-independence African story depicted a strange leadership relay that fielded dynasties, monarchies, autocrats, militarists and democracies. In Togo, the Eyademas ruled for over 50 years after a military coup by Gnassingbe Eyadema. In Gabon, Omar Bongo ruled for almost 42 years and handed over to his son till the coup of August, 2023. Angola has Jose Eduardo dos Santos chalking 36 years in power, just like Teodoro Obiang Mbiango of Equatorial Guinea. Robert Mugabe spent not less than 35 years as President in Zimbabwe, while Paul Biya of Cameroon stayed on for 32 years+. In the Congo, Sassou Nguesso spent 31 years against Yoweri Museveni's 30+ years in Uganda.

Similarly, Constitutions were changed by incumbent presidents for selfish interests. Examples include Yoweri Museveni of Uganda, Faure Gnassingbe of Togo, Paul Biya of Cameroon, Paul Kagame of Rwanda, Alassane Ouattara of Ivory Coast, Ismail Omar Guelleh of Djibouti, Abdoulaye Wade of Senegal, Azali Assoumani of Comoros, Guinea's

Alpha Condé, Denis Sassou Nguesso of Congo Republic, Pierre Nkurunziza of Burundi, and Idriss Deby of Chad. In 2024, President Macky Sall of Senegal delayed the national election in an effort to extend his tenure of office. He was however, overruled by the Constitutional Council for the election to take place and subsequent election of President Bassirou Diomaye Faye. In 2024, Togo changed from a presidential universal adult suffrage system to a parliamentary system which effectively took away the rights of the citizens to directly elect their leader. The list of constitutional manipulation by ruling presidents and majority parties in Africa goes on and on.

There were attempts (some successful) in Zimbabwe, the Democratic Republic of Congo, Kenya, Gabon, and South Africa to perpetuate the presidency with cronies or family members when the political "Methuselahs" had to leave. The claim by these power-drunk leaders that they were practicing democracy is confounding. Does a functional multi-party constitutional democracy permit the manipulation of tenure of office to favor an individual? No! The standard practice the world over is two terms, but the number of years per term differs from country to country. Is it not strange for such African leaders to manipulate the law that brought them into office, yet claim they are democrats? It is in place to say that they rather, carry out constitutional coup d'état and descend into the realms of monarchs and dictators.

Plato, in the book "The Republic" chastised democracy for its lack of resilience (reliance on majority rule) and unbridled rights of freedom on which it rests its moral values. It becomes a rational or irrational tool to produce a leader for the masses so long as they identify with the candidate and bank their hopes on him to satisfy them. Who then are the masses? They are people who, by ordering of society, are classified as occupiers of the lower rungs on the ladder of prominence. Often, they constitute the majority of the population and belong to the working class who travail for their superiors for pay. They are poor, have low/average educational qualifications, are moderately cultured, unexposed, and often go through life without adequate security. They are challenged to soldier on and break into the middle class or the high class.

This kind of social ordering is unknown in indigenous African system. From ancient Rome to medieval Europe, and today's Western World, social stratification (low class, middle class, and upper class) is deeply anchored on materiality where wealth holds sway. No wonder, 'The Donald' as reported by CNN at the Duluth, Minnesota rally in June 2018, threw a challenge by saying,

[*"... the elite, the elite, why are they elite? I have much better apartment than they do. I am smarter than they are. I am richer than they are. I became President, and they didn't."*]

The lot of the masses has been a struggle for a better life, to move away from the lower rungs and have control over their own affairs amidst the economic snares of the rich. It is, however, puzzling that in instances where anyone of them broke into the middle or upper class, he tends to "look down" upon his former class mates as if there is a normative in his new circle of friends to do so. The political and democratic rights for the masses is limited to decision-making about who should become their leader and exercise sovereignty of the state on their behalf.

In today's world of universal adult suffrage, the masses crave to establish an identity with a presidential candidate in ideas, thoughts and actions. So an astute person, adept at pragmatism, popularity and having the financial means can endear himself to them by appropriate messaging to seal the deal. The issue of whether the individual has acumen to function within laid down constitutional checks and balances is more or less a secondary matter for the political gold digger. The priority is to attain the presidency first. It does not matter who or what you are, what you know or do, where you come from, your color, parentage, or belief. Leave those for the masses to decide. And that is democracy- the acclaimed restorer of equality of all people. But the equality is more about political rights, not the bread and butter issues that brought about social stratification and the political system in the first place.

Historically, democracy like other political arrangements, has not adequately tackled the bread and butter issues. It gives power to the grassroots, and invariably, consolidates the gains of a well-knitted wealthy class. It professes opportunities for the commons and leaves the decision to be made by the middle and upper classes. It invites the people to cast votes, to elect who will represent them in matters that affect their livelihoods, but not for the people to directly determine how the resources should be generated and apportioned in collective interest. It assures things will be better in the future while the masses remain troubled about the hardships of today. And that is democracy?

Political arrangements are to foster good governance by meeting the competing interest and aspirations of people in a given territory. So far, democracy has not proven itself as the only capable system to do so. Governance systems such as monarchies, dynasties, and one-party states have also shown results in livelihood enhancement.

It is a cliché that a child goes through developmental stages to maturation, and at every stage, certain critical faculties are developed to complete his being. During adulthood, the person becomes matured and capable of leading an independent life with limited or no external support. Imagine a parent who abandoned the child or forcibly tried to induce him to become independent a few years after birth. He would have done a grievous disservice to the child by truncating his developmental process. The growth pattern and experience of individuals collectively, indicate the developmental stage reached by that society and central to the type of governance system most suitable for them.

In Africa today, parroted multi-party democracy has become the regime. It is rated by the West as the best governance system for the continent. It is imbibed and consequently enshrined in the constitutions of many countries. Periodically, people vote to elect their leaders. The presidential candidates are required to stand on the ticket of a political party or stand as independent candidates. The pains of democracy show that independent candidature is a major task; the amount of resources and efforts required are overwhelming. Whereas sitting presidents (who often run for a second term) have no problems renewing their mandate internally, it is a different ball game when they are to contest against opposition candidates from other parties in a general election. The situation becomes more intense when the presidential candidates are all new in a fresh election.

A cocktail of political trappings such as negotiation, influence-peddling, lobbying, arm-twisting, revolts, truth-avoidance, diplomacy, insults, votes buying, wealth flaunting, cajoling, sweet-talking, character assassination, wild promises, image building and rebranding, popularity drive, and even black-mail are adopted by the candidates to outsmart or dent the reputation of others.

Democracy repudiates unethical conduct during campaigns but has little power to stop it. Instead, it leaves the moral judgment to the people, who are already divided along political lines. The strong desire to win the next elections often "blindfolds" political parties as they try to rally together against their opponents regardless of any internal wrangling. An avalanche of "democratic" attacks are hurled at one another, sometimes ferocious as to engulf society at large. Homes are torn apart, ethnic groups against ethnic groups, men against men, and the learned against the learned are the ruins in the campaign tracks. It is common to hear in the news physical attacks and the loss of innocent lives. Often, tempers rise so high that the fears of war linger. In effect, society becomes fractured, characterized by the "we" versus "them" syndrome.

If the election is to contest a sitting president, then the opposition party has a more arduous task. The government (in the face of ineffective accountability, checks, and balances) would often plunder state resources as part of a general scheme to gain advantage, shackle, and prevent the opposition party from gaining power. In doing this, officials exert some control over state media and other media houses that they purposefully established to promote their agenda.

The trend in political inducement of late is for governments to grant broadcast operating license to favorites. The behind-the-scene condition demands they report favorably in exchange of juicy advertisements, contracts, promotional activities, and even representation in the seat of government. In addition, opulent material benefits are given influential journalists who aligned with the government.

The maneuvers of a biased media and politically tainted journalists include (i) waging a "psychological war" against opposition parties to the advantage of the sitting government (ii) massaging the facts by adulterating the truth (iii) creating popular resentment against opposition leaders they detest (iv) superficial analysis of public policy impacts of government initiatives (v) creating fun around important livelihood issues that do not serve the political interest of the government (vi) deliberate distortion to deceive or confuse or hide the facts from public scrutiny. Their action goes against the noble roles assigned to them by the Constitution as the watchdog to protect the public interest, and resources. They are expected to be investigative, analytical, fair, factual, impersonal, and accountable.

Electoral Commissions

The role of Electoral Commissions in the democratic electioneering process is critical. They are mandated to be the referee whose neutrality should not only be deemed legally but perceived as such by all parties. How they perform their statutory and civic responsibility, without doubt, will indicate whether a political party has fairly and legally won an election to assume authority and form a government. In this regard, many African countries have guarded their electioneering processes by laws and regulations. Across the board, they are independent bodies and their modus operandi are not subject to external control. Ironically, the mode of appointment of the members especially, the Head and Board of Directors is by the Executive Arm of the State (the President), which to some extent, reverses the supposed independence. The dangers of appointment and some discretions that can be exercised by the President over Electoral Commissions are many;

   i.   appointment of party loyalists and cronies;

  ii.   removal of perceived non-loyalists;

 iii.   manipulation of the electioneering process through selectivity, voter suppression, gerrymandering, deploying security services to frustrate voters in opposition strong holds, creating additional territories and election reporting channels.

The extent of the independence of an Electoral Commission is unclear and there is the danger of dictatorship since the entity under a bad leadership can become non-transparent, non-accountable, partisan and authoritarian. Also, the actions of the Commission may lead to negative public perception and lack of trust in the electioneering process. This is a very serious situation because it is the sovereignty of the people that serves as a check on the Executive Arm of government. Thus, any attempt to deprive them from exercising their franchise is tantamount to a coup d'état. Many electoral disputes are blamable on the poor performance of Electoral Commissions as a result of bias, inaccurate results, executive manipulation and the lack of transparency before, during, and after elections. Examples include Malawi (2020), Kenya (2023, 2017), Nigeria (2023), and Ghana (2020, 2012). The attempt to create a truly independent Electoral Commission is herculean but, when the electioneering process is clearly defined (in a blueprint) and owned by all parties, it is most likely that the outcome will be without acrimony. The resort to the Judiciary to adjudicate on election matters is appropriate but does not heal wounds. Where the balance of power is skewed in favor of the Executive Arm, it is more likely the courts cannot be independent and make objective rulings. In the face of the mentioned factors it can be said that the effectiveness of Electoral Commissions in Africa hinges on decentralization, a high degree of transparency, accountability and ownership creation throughout the electioneering process.

Social Media and Information Technology

In as much as modern mass communication tools, platforms, and services have become push factors for individual choices, they have invariably served as mechanisms for manipulating innocent citizens and influencing democratic election results in a predetermined manner. The transformation from opaque ballot boxes to transparent and electronic ones in some African countries inured to the benefit of opposition parties since it facilitated transparency and their coming into power. Nonetheless, the revelations ascribed to the 2016 US elections about the diabolical use of private information of Facebook subscribers in a so-called psychographic modeling technique by Cambridge Analytica indicts the sacrosanctity of functional democracy. To what extent can it be called democratic when voters' data are compiled, analyzed, tweaked, and directed to influence voting behavior? Is it prudent for one party to score advantages (discreetly or indiscreetly) over the other before and during the elections by voter manipulation? That there are limited ways for the democratic state to exercise checks and balances against such occurrences shows that democracy has processual flaws and might not be the ready answer to many governance and livelihood issues after all.

Generally, aside from irrationality in voter behavior, the campaign to win votes itself is insufficient on the bread and butter issues. Instead, a fusion of peripheral considerations come to the fore and dominate campaign messages. Even where a political party has a manifesto, it is hardly read and understood by the masses. The political plots and schemes regrettably, are publicized more often which tends to increase tension in African societies in many ways.

Ethnicity

There are over a thousand ethnic groups across Africa, each with its own local language and unique culture. Each country has an ethnic agglomeration whose members have a strong identity and attachment. It is easy to identify the large and the dominant ones that have features such as territorial advantage, economic viability, an average to high educational attainment, religious identity, social and cultural cohesion and pride, and popularity.

The major ethnic group(s) tends to dominate politically and economically to the disadvantage of the smaller ones, who, in appreciation of their vulnerability, coalesce in support of a popular candidate. This balancing act serves as a check on the unrestrained political rise of one large ethnic group. It, however, stands that the astute politician can win political power by mobilizing people from the majority ethnic group and moderate votes from minority ones. It becomes less daunting if the declaration of the winner at general elections is by a simple majority rather than the Electoral College system akin to the USA. Although noted with federal systems, African democracies should explore the possibility of adapting the Electoral College. It has the advantages to (i) negate marginalization of certain parts or minority groups (ii) reduce ethnicity in elections (iii) lessen electoral disputes about the total number of votes counted or the call for national recount (iv) fine-tune governance and leadership discourse (v) shift the discussions to area-specific developmental issues beyond ethnic or religious affiliation (vi) compel politicians to look for ways to promote national cohesion and regional balance rather than concentrating efforts at densely populated areas or ethnic groups for popular votes.

Religious Fraternity

The African has a strong religious attachment based on his worldview about life and the after-death phenomenon. Be it African Traditional Religion, Christianity, or Islam, the African never ceases to identify with members of his religious group. He will do whatever it takes to make himself known and live peaceably with other fraternities. So, the astute politician first seeks to endear himself to his religious base and later rebrands himself to appeal to other religious sects. He does tantalizing publicity by any means possible to be spoken well of. Later, he will maneuver into another populous and influential religious group with gestures that are well publicized. He will not hesitate to build alliances and make commitments, especially in selecting a running mate among them in an effort to blend religion at the head of government. This strategy hardly fails in countries like Nigeria and Ghana.

Generational Syndrome and Community of Friends

Generally, the African leadership trajectory shows that the leaders come from one generation to another. Excepting military dictatorship, the post-independent leaders were born in certain periods. For example, people above 60 years were born before independence and went through distinct upbringing, tutelage, and experience that more or less distinguish them from those who were born after independence. From their school days to working life, people of certain generation have their peculiarities, built networks and companionship that eventually influence their leadership style. If the orientation in the pre-independence generational period is to mimic the white man, then it is more likely that the African leader, by reconditioning, will likely seek the company of fellows of same nature. By extension, he is likely going to be out of touch with people of a different generation. Perhaps having a robust database of influential "old school" fellows is one of the ways to wield political clout.

Business Contacts

Multi-party democracy is capital-intensive, and the business community is a major source of finance. In the real sense the funds that they provide to political parties are never a "gift" or mere "donation" but an investment in the short, medium or long term. Surely, they will find a means to recoup through business deals. Who are the business community? They are the people who, more or less fit the description given aristocrats. They own the factors and means of production of goods and services. Their ultimate end is to make profit. They control labor (in essence, the livelihood of the masses) just like in the olden days of Europe. Even as they invest in political parties, the astute ones double-edged their investments beyond a single political party. Be it the ruling or opposition party that emerges as the winner at the polls, the business class remains on the winning side.

International Goodwill

Elections in Africa are melting pots for international attention and influence peddling. There have always been attempts by foreign governments and institutions to influence votes by simulation, withholding or advancing funds to sitting government, secret meetings with preferred political parties, public statements, research and publication of survey reports, and material support, sometimes through religious bodies, NGOs, and CSOs. Most often, governments that incur the displeasure of the international community suffer at the polls through these maneuvers. So the African politician strives to win the hearts and minds of the international community by any means possible, sometimes conflicting the party manifesto or interest of citizens.

Popularity and Appeal to the Masses

Democracy has scant room for analysis of the competence and experience of candidates. Often, what matters most is popularity. While the issues of policy and capacity become the concern of the learned class, the masses having no such level of enlightenment, look for things in a candidate including stature and physical appearance, flair in speech, presence at religious and social events, sense of humor, properties owned, and genealogy. Often, inadequate attention is given to the capacity of a candidate to deliver on his promises. And for whatever reason, the masses stick with populist ideas and catchy campaign slogans and phrases. So, to become successful, the astute politician will profile the masses, their preferences and tailor campaign messages accordingly. Victory beckons!

Vote Buying

Poverty is an entrapment and the good that people know they ought to do they are unable to do. It takes courage and uprightness to uphold the truth under trying moments when the illusions of materiality descends. The morally corrupt politician knows very well that the people are poor and lacked material things. He, indecently, sees it as an opportunity to do a trade-off with their sovereignty by offering them material things in exchange for votes. The susceptible citizen also knows that it is only during election periods that he is most likely to derive personal gains from the politician directly. So, the underlying principle of democracy, the will of the people is monetized or given away for material benefit. This action is a slur on good governance because it leads to non-accountability regarding how politicians acquire wealth and their responsiveness to tax obligations. Most importantly, vote buying undermines the core values of democracy and if necessary, should be outlawed in a new African governance ethos.

Deception of the Masses?

To answer this question one has to look at the character and culture of the origin of democracy. It emerged as a form of political regime that opposes the abuse of power by a leader and embraces the equality of rights. History reveals that Europe was built through enslavement and tribute. Most of the infrastructural work was done by slaves. It implies that at every point in time, there was the master and the slave, the Lord and the servant.

It does no harm to conclude that wealth, to a large extent determined who was a ruler. Moreover, the states/lords fought among themselves to conquer and dominate the vanquished. Some positive societal changes emerged from the wars; for instance, class equality was established by the Athenians during the Persian Wars when the aristocrats lost control of wealth and the power over people. In the process, a new thought of oneness developed among the citizenry. Later, this sense of equality of rights was subdued when the Roman Empire ascended. The aristocrats re-emerged with their unbridled passion for wealth, slaves, and position.

Compared to the Greeks, the Romans brought back the alignment of politics, rights, and wealth for a number of years. The participation in political decision-making was, largely determined by status, nobility (wealth), religious influence, and military power. For many years the aristocrats held onto power in the cities. The art of representation (which afforded the masses the opportunity for political expression) was a later development. It was done to win the support of the wealthy class who were not resident in the major cities. It was feared that they could mobilize the masses and wage war against the establishment in the capital city. Thus, they were invited as representatives of the commoners and, by so doing, the aristocrats provided security for themselves.

The main issue is that the hoi polloi were deemed the third estate after the nobles and the religious class. They are the taxpayers, the day-by-day operational people whose sweat and toil to earn a living has always been at the dictate of the wealthy class. The other remarkable change that Europe later made in increasing the voting space was to adopt universal suffrage, where all qualified people in the territory (including women) could participate regardless of economic power or being an adult male.

Universal suffrage is upheld and practiced steadfastly according to the principles and fundamentals that recognize the dignity of all. Its elements comprise civil rights / human rights (relative to freedoms of expression, association, property-owning, et cetera), equal right to vote, separation of powers and the independence of the organs of state (especially the Judiciary), and religious freedom. Regardless of these rights, it cannot be firmly concluded that democracy has successfully tackled the butter and bread issues of the masses.

In the Western world, democracy stands firmly on individual responsibility and rights conferred in law. It is no respecter of persons, but thrives on the issues which to be thoroughly discussed, demands the exercise of analytical mind. Democracy imposes responsibility on practitioners to stand for their rights, be assertive, and insist the law, as far as practicable, should be the final arbiter. To cut corners around democracy is to try being ahead of the law, which is not an easy thing to do. Hence, actions of people should be within the law and be guided by ethics, often taught in homes, schools, workplaces, and communities.

The tenet is that ALL are EQUAL in RIGHTS as given by the Creator. Whatever difference there is among people is due to nurture factors. So far as they (the nurture factors) become detrimental, solutions are needed to enable each individual to pursue his God-given talent. In that regard, social interventions are required from government to address the basic welfare needs of all especially, the disadvantaged and the vulnerable. The objective is to identify economic and social needs as factors in the exercise of rights. It is to promote equitable development and for everyone to be impacted, yet in varying degrees depending on the means and efforts of the individual.

In building an enlightened society, having the appropriate Western personality, the young ones are trained to think deep in the abstract (reasoning about the issue) and permitted to tell their parents that they disagree with them on a subject matter, and there will be no disharmony in the family. The subordinate will express his views in contrast with his superior and will not be worried about victimization. Nobody feels like being on cloud nine because of title or position. For the same reason, the politician is willing to be held accountable for his promises and actions, and when found wanting, will step down with a sincere apology. That is the power of Western democracy. It fits into the personality and character of the Western World.

Compare this Western culture to an African society that frowns on individuality, and from childhood, the education of the young ones is to enable them to think communally first, where one does not readily acquire the independence and fortitude to analyze issues devoid of the persona. So, depending on how the situation plays out, it is likely that family and friends will be excused while a foe will be sanctioned for the same wrongful conduct. Similarly, the principles of democracy are interpreted and applied to personal, ethnic or partisan advantage. This is at variance with democratic principles, built on the values of impersonality, fairness, justice, and equity.

Look at an African society where the title promotes (more or less) the personality, even when his psycho-motor-affective nature does not meet the standards of the office. Again, think of a society that sees the apology of a leader as a sign of weakness and a disgrace. So, when politicians in office drain public resources through various "camouflage" policies, it is not necessarily considered wrong; there are people who will always come out to defend the wrongful act. Is it not strange to hear people postulating that appropriation is a character of public office and should be expected in African society? As is the case nowadays, any attempt by a new government to prosecute past officials is readily, tagged as a witch-hunt. The main issues hardly received the needed attention. Good governance is not about the position or title of office but the issue, what is prescribed in law and sanctified by morality.

The issue is distinct from and has nothing to do with the personality or material possessions. That is why when Martin Luther

King Jr. proclaimed in his, "I have a Dream," that speech is generally accepted as the dynamic energy for American power, prosperity, and progress. The ideals he espoused resonated among enlightened people regardless of lineage, color, class, race, and wealth. Unfortunately, the issue of what is good and just and ought to be done is yet to receive adequate appreciation in African democracy.

Since the 1990s, how to build a prosperous society from multi-party democracy remains a tall order. The continent has a high illiteracy rate that has negatively impacted the enlightenment of the people and the efforts to create a pool of critical minds. Where there exists some potentials, governments have not made concerted efforts to identify and build the enabling environment for them to develop. Look at a society where the constitution/laws are virtually unknown to the vast majority, where it seems it is only those who went to law schools who should be concerned. Meanwhile, the requirement for a successful democracy is the rule of law. In its absence, how well can multi-party democracy truly change and raise the narratives of the masses? So, the people should know their civic rights and responsibilities.

Beyond the weak spread of governance knowledge among the people, look at the low investment and deprivation of the Judiciary in many African countries. Aside from the infrequent attempts to modernize the laws, leaders in Africa have not taken the trouble to make the Judiciary truly independent; they deprive it of the needed resources and make it dependent on them. In how many countries are the budgets of the Judiciary sent directly to the people's representatives in Parliament for approval and subsequent resource allocation without the impediments of a frustrating intervening ministry? What will possibly make the Judiciary truly independent and effective may not rest only on fair and just application of the laws, but the enabling environment and conditions of service to serve God and country.

The powers, protection, and privileges conferred on African leaders are beyond belief. Some of them are contradictory to the tenets of democracy and are bad examples. One of them is the exemption of a leader from paying taxes while citizens are required to pay. The questionable privileges make them look like dictators and monarchs clothed in democratic robes. Is there an African leader who will take the bull by the horn, and ask, "Does my working condition reflect the true situation of remuneration in the public sector?"

The adulterated "African-by-Nature and European-by-Nurture," by following the Western Governance Model takes hold of the pecks of the colonial office, and begins to implement portions of the laws that come along with privileges. He would not take the pain to create or align it to his home situation. He would just copy it. Neither would he do any intelligent work about what is suitable for his environment but rather focuses on what gives him an advantage over others. Yet he proclaims with a gusto that he is practicing democracy. So, when it comes to human rights (for instance, the rights of gays, lesbians, bisexuals, et cetera), he would regress to African traditional values, proclaiming that it is not an African way of life. So, aspects of democracy are un-African? Fair enough. One will wish the avidity with which some parts of Western democracy are identified as un-African, will be extended to other areas to deepen socio-cultural and economic development the African way.

Even as the hobbling between original African practices and Western democratic requirements continues, the African leader has the luxury to do as he desires. After all, he has adequate protection in a Western-styled constitution, and the imbalance in cross-institutional accountability adds to the list of advantages at his behest. He relies on a pitiable value system that seeks to say, "It does not matter what he says or does not say, what he does or does not do." He feels reinforced so long as the support of party members, sympathizers, and cronies abound. They will not flip and are ready to defend him anyhow, anytime, anywhere.

Even where it was self-evident that the leader has gone wrong morally and even constitutionally, the identification with him, and the "we-feeling" are so strong that followers would rather be on the attack against those who pointed out the wrong. The leader's shame is their shame. If they even have to concede that he was wrong, they would, for party unity and victory at the polls, find a way to defend him. When they go on rebuttal, they will refer to the records of the opposition party (if it had ever been in power) and individuals saying, "You are no better, you did similar or worse things in your time." Is this reasonable? How can something wrong in the past justify a current wrong? Were people enlightened and democratic institutions working well, such statements and repeat of unlawful or immoral conduct by leaders would not be on the rise.

So many factors give discretion to the African leader to the point that his words do not necessarily oblige him before the people, especially when the leader has a weak moral courage to live by and defend what is good, fair, and just. A leader cannot stand for the right when within himself, an aspect and commitment to that right is not there. The crux of the matter here is that the discerning leader means what he says and is measured in his utterances. Some African leaders have shown the way (e.g. Kwame Nkrumah and Nelson Mandela), and there is no reason to think others cannot do so. But for now, too much power, discretion, and resources in the hands of African leaders, intermingled with their unrealistic promises to the people should be a source of concern or lesson to Neo-Africans.

Lurking Military Juntas

To date, the juicy promises of democracy to Africans remain elusive. When the Bretton Woods institutions prescribed it as the best governance model in the 1980s, little did African elites read into it to detect that the underlying motivation was to protect Western interests and control African resources in a planned manner. The Economic Restructuring Programs and related support systems aimed at bailing out African governments from economic and financial hardships (which the West had a hand in creating in the first place) was a strategy. They knew that the critical factors for a successful democratic practice were absent among Africans, especially the enlightenment of the people. But they were keen to implant it, knowing that once governments signed off and committed to constitutional democracy, the deal was sealed in their interest. As for how it was practiced, that is a matter for Africans; the West could not care much.

Democracy creates security for external investors whose levels of resources for investment, Africans do not have and cannot afford. The capitalists flock in and explore the quick-win economic areas that are often capital-intensive sectors such as energy, oil and gas, mining, construction, and manufacturing. They coerce African governments for special privileges such as tax incentives (holidays and exemptions), increased expatriate quotas, and free zones. Often, the promises of increased jobs and improved living standards for the people do not materialize. In effect, the economic impacts of democracy do not reflect on the quality of life of the people, who are left to find their own mechanisms to cope with their dissatisfaction, frustration, and anger. The World Bank (2023) mentioned a reduction in economic growth in sub-Saharan Africa from 3.6% in 2022 to 3.1 in 2023.

After four decades of experimental democracy, the military juntas are staging a comeback, to capture power from democratically elected leaders. The wind in the sail of democracy is getting snuffed in Africa and the West cannot hold back their disappointment. In a spate of four years (2020-2023), there were ten attempted coups in West and Central Africa. Some of them were successful in overthrowing the governments. For example, President Ibrahim Boubacar Keita in Mali (2020), President Alpha Conde in Guinea (2021), Lieutenant Colonel Paul-Henri Sandaogo Damiba (who was a coup maker) in Burkina Faso (2021), Mohammed Bazoum of Niger (2023), and Ali Bongo in

Gabon (2023). The number could increase if solutions are not found to the problems often used to justify the putsch by juntas, namely;

- electoral fraud and consequent stealing of the sovereign will of the people by the sitting government with the connivance of Electoral Commission;

- opulence (of sitting president, family, friends, and associates) while the majority of citizens loiter in extreme poverty;
- mismanagement of the country's resources which has led to abject poverty among the people; and
- ineffective security which exposed the citizens to danger, harassment, and loss of lives and property.

Much against democratic expectations, the people of the affected countries jubilated and cheered on the military leaders. Why? Two factors stand out:

i.   many African leaders are finding it hard to live by democratic principles – some have lost the cardinal values of integrity, accountability, and transparency of decisions and actions;

ii. the people are not getting any dividends from democracy. The resultant apathy does not empower anybody to boldly defend democracy.

CHAPTER FIVE

Draining the African Swamp

["Africa is rich but not poor ... it is Africans who are poor, not Africa"]
Kwame Nkrumah's Address at the Conference of African Freedom

Fighters in Accra, 4th June, 1962

If over 30% of the world's resources are in Africa, there can be no justification for Africans to be poor, except the leaders are weak and unable to win big deals for their people. What the West, and for that matter the rest of the world, is looking for is not necessarily who is the African leader and what governance system is practiced. Their focus is more on who protects their investment and economic interest. Examples exist; they do massive business with so-called authoritarian China, do the same in the monarchical Arab countries, and support dictatorial governments whose leaders are discreetly in bed with them.

As The Donald said during his address to the UN General Assembly on 19th September, 2017, *"...We do not expect diverse countries to share the same cultures, traditions, or even systems of government, but we do expect all nations to uphold these two core sovereign duties, to respect the interests of their own people and the rights of every other sovereign nation."*

The United States won independence from Britain and charted its own unique republican constitutional path, and it has been working for them. Great Britain remained in its constitutional democracy, carving a role for the monarchy, and it does work for them. China, and for that matter, Russia have their unique governance system, which is yielding results for them too. All these countries do business with one another, and life goes on.

If the governance system is the determinant, why would Western countries be engaged in business with non-democratic states? It is all about what promotes and consolidates their interest. This position has never changed since it was propounded during the Berlin Conference (1884-1885) to partition Africa and pave way for Western domination. The countries gathered included the United Kingdom, France, Portugal, Belgium, Spain, the German Empire, Netherlands, Denmark, Italy, Austria-Hungary, Sweden-Norway, the Ottoman Empire, the Russian Empire and the United States.

During the 4-month or so period of scheming to share what was not theirs, the appetitive behavior by the 14 countries (except the witness and power to abstain of the United States) was not to consider the launch of a popular governance system for Africa. Their strongest motivation was to (i) stop fighting among themselves in the quest of African resources and (ii) consolidate economic gains on the continent along the European Model. No more, no less!

They instituted an adulterated governance system as the vessel to exploit economic resources and control Africans. They created positions, which were occupied by themselves to steer the affairs of Africans. It worked for them, and for many years they have had their way. The continental independence struggles succeeded in obviating their authority and official positions. But the foundations upon which their governance and administrative systems were built remain virtually unchanged. That is how far the independence struggle has gone. Is it worthwhile?

Africa cannot afford to enter the next century, an epoch of intense global competition and cooperation, from a beggarly position. That conduct does not win any respect and dignity among civilized nations of the world. The African leaders of old have laid the foundation by restoration of political power. Their efforts to lift up Africans from poverty and deprivation were only at the rudimentary phase when their regimes ended or became abortive. The time has come for continental leaders of today and tomorrow to rededicate themselves to the strenuous work of leadership and work harder for Economic Empowerment and Wealth Creation for Africans. There are remarkable stories of countries colonized in the past but have become big players on the world stage today. Look at the Asian Tigers. How did their leaders do it? How about the United States? Was it not a British colony? It means there can be a turnaround if Neo-African leaders take time to develop themselves, put their shoulders to the wheel, and work for the people. It means there can be a turnaround if Neo-African leaders take time to develop themselves, put their shoulders to the wheel and work for the people.

Deconstruction of the African Psyche

There is a fierce urgency to put off Africans from the dependency mentality to a new self-reliance and "can do" consciousness. This is because Africans are best-positioned to solve their own problems just as other nations solve theirs. External support is facilitative but should not replace home-grown indigenous solutions. The starting point is essentially education (both formal and informal) of the youth. The focus should be on developing the mind (through logic and reasoning, values, and skills). What should be discouraged is the perpetuation of the shallow and skewed educational system that does not practically relate Africans to their immediate environments but those of other countries.

A new wave of learning should permeate the continent, which, among others, should encourage African History across educational curricula for the African to know who he is, past, present, and future. African leaders should develop continental think-tanks and personalities whose deeds and capacities are towards landmark international recognition. The prime objective is to inculcate "first love for Africa in the African," and successfully position him to demonstrate his talents universally.

African leaders should see this as a leadership function in addition to solving the butter and bread issues. It is so because the silver lining of development is in the psyche. A positive mindset is the propeller of sustainable development. Its deficiency has been a drag on the collective progress of Africans for far too long. Many clubs, unions, associations, and civil society groups keep educating people about the good tidings of Western multi-party democracy. That is not bad but can the servant be greater than the master in the master's house? Africa cannot claim to be equal or better practitioners of Western democracy than the West. Thus, African leaders should reflect and ask themselves what has happened to the machinery for raising the consciousness of Africans? What happened to the Pan-African Movement? Has it been sacrificed on the altar of political expediency? Should it not be reactivated and rebranded? Is it not a fallacy to think that because Independence Day is celebrated, Africans are free? No, it is not wholly true. As Dr Kwame Nkrumah puts it,

["*it is only the outward forms that have changed but the substance of colonialism remains just the same.*"]

Talking about a new mindset for Africans goes beyond militant views regarding the colonialists and the effects of colonialism. It should be more about the African's worldview of life and the need to internalize positive values that spite greed, ignorance, corruption, disorderliness, unassertiveness, indiscipline, et cetera. The deconstruction of the negative mindset is the key to individual and collective progress as re-echoed during the 1957 Independence Day in Ghana when the leader called for transition into a new positive orientation - the realization that Africans are no more colonial but free and independent people.

Security, Peace and Unity

Africans have a birthright to unite for which reason the political forbears delivered inspirational speeches to outline the strategies and plans that should be pursued. Peace and security are pivotal to every deliverable of life; socio-economic, financial, infrastructural, livelihood and empowerment. Without it, Africans cannot harness their strengths but will continue to suffer the downward trends in living conditions.

The Planning Committee of the AU Arts Festival (2018) puts it thus,

[*"We also want to remind us all the need to be united as one people. True African unity and sovereignty can only be gained through a united front where we allow economies of scale and free movement of people, goods and services to empower us economically and politically. These would help us to stand up to the dictates of the West and other economic powers that always wish to pursue their own interests in their interventions on the continent."*]

The call to unite should not be left at the behest of only African leaders but owned by people within and beyond the continent. There should be a big push to educate Africans about the relevance and importance of security, peace, and unity for continental transformation. Indubitably, intra-country conflicts constitute the greatest threat to the realization of this dream. Many of the fractures come from faulty governance arrangements, defective electioneering processes and failure to resort to courts for adjudication. African countries that have made progress in keeping the peace can serve as catalysts; Ghana (2021), Kenya (2023), Nigeria (2023), are examples.

The African Union is alive and doing its best towards continental progress but needs a re-orientation to deliver on the dreams of those who toiled for its establishment. Compared to 1950s and 1960s, the dynamics have changed over the years, and there is the need to re-examine the relevance of the fundamental values set by the founding fathers and determine whether they trend with developments in the modern world, especially, technological advancement and economic order. To some extent, the original ethos underlying the Union is challenged in the face of increasing globalization.

The advocacy for "unity" does not mean Africa should operate as a single jurisdictional body - under one President like the United States. No! The sovereignty of the people in the various countries will make it challenging to have one continental state or government at this time.

The unity should be aligned with identification, unique preferences, and commonality of policies. In this regard, African countries should have, as much as possible, policy re-alignment and coordinating offices that will promote cross-cutting and mutually beneficial interventions / practices. Although there might be slight variations (because of peculiar country cases), Africa has the advantage to be recognized as one block on pertinent global issues. More importantly, it will be easier for the people in the various countries to link up and relate to one another.

Continental Economic Empowerment

The Western model for economic development has been prioritized since independence and the result is where Africa is today – a sad story of abject poverty. The prescription for unlocking economic development on the continent is not to stimulate comparative advantage but to divert the outcomes of the competitive advantage externally. As a result, African governments keep looking outside for budgetary support. Annually, foreign governments and institutions shore up African countries. Without this support, many governments cannot survive.

The trend ought to change. A new approach is required since the repeated doing of the same thing using the same formula will not yield any different result. Something new has to happen using a common sense approach to development. Africa has to unlock itself from within using an overarching philosophy of "Africa First," which seeks to prioritize the internalization of continental resources for Africans. It will be a "tough strategy" to uphold since some commitments (agreements and contracts) have been made (and potential threats exist for foreign countries), and Africa is already in a web of debt.

Self-dependency is a common character in the history of countries that are considered powerful today. Examples include the United States, Russia, Europe, China, India, Brazil, Japan, and the Asian Tigers. It is a cardinal value that Africa should embrace. Just as a child, in the beginning, is carried about, and later, crawls before tottering from one point to the other in quest of target, there comes a time when he must eventually walk by himself. Africa has a lot to learn including how to move away from her unprofitable trade with external countries to intra-continental trade. The continent was subdued by trade, and it is by trade that it would attain economic power. The good news is that a lot of the resources the world needs abound in the region.

The boost in trade as a catalyst to economic freedom is critical because the records show that intra-continental trade is negligible and Africans are rather creating wealth elsewhere for other people. For example, whereas trade among African countries amounts to a paltry 11% in 2015, that for European Union members is 70%. Is it the making of the colonialists that African leaders are failing to increase trade among themselves? No! It is the decades-old failure to have a workable intra-continental trade framework and strategy. Any single African country that tries to strike a trade deal with powerful foreign countries will be the ultimate loser. In addition, that action will undermine the collective interest of Africans. It is therefore commendable that in 2018, African leaders took the bold step at the 28th Ordinary Session of the Assembly of the African Union, and agreed the commencement of the African Continental Free Trade Agreement (AfCFTA) headquartered in Accra, Ghana.

The Agreement is deemed the critical junction for import/export trajectory, planning, and budgets of member countries. It would be appropriate to back roll-out plans with clear trade and business information that seek to mobilize resources especially, from African-led businesses and encourage them to do business in Africa. It means there should be trade reforms in member countries that guarantee the security of investment, attractive returns on investment, competitive prices, and incentives. Member countries should have branch offices that link aspects of their national plans and actions to AfCFTA strategies. To this end, results-focused and dedicated experts should develop the necessary policies and programs that will facilitate investment from the private sector.

Even as the AfCFTA began (with expected initial challenges), African leaders should review the competitive advantages they have in existing agreements and weed out the unprofitable ones provided the potential and opportunity exist. It should be a continental tactic that should be carried out within realistic timelines. As Africa internalizes the utilization of its resources, the essence is not to degrade any foreign investor but to send the message that Africa deserves better deals. The AfCFTA should not only secure the interest of its members but guard against any member losing economically relative to trade offers from external competitors. Its members should be supported so that they can offer competitive prices for their products and services on the world market.

For certainty, the promotion of intra-continental trade cannot be restrictive because the world has become so interrelated in the provision, and consumption of goods and services. Certain procurements would have to come from outside. The AfCFTA should look at the imports/exports of African countries and advise whether or not the goods and services are procurable from within. There should be incentives or a league that annually rewards countries that topped in intra-continental trade and procurement.

The records show that a bouquet of African imports in the past years was predominantly food, clothing, stationary, automotive vehicles, pharmaceuticals, telecom equipment (including mobile phones), electronics, computers, and IT products. Even though there are unique country conditions, generally, the importation of items from other continents can be reduced or replaced progressively when African countries produce them on a large scale and at affordable prices. It means that there should be a major push to prioritize (i) industrialization in specific sectors and (ii) transfer of technology as a requirement for foreign direct investment.

Since independence, home-grown industrialization has been a work in progress. It seems the continent does not have adequate technical, managerial, investment, and human resources to manage the complexity. Many reasons account for this. Key among them is the philosophy behind post-independence industrialization. For whatever reasons, many African governments accepted the economic mantra that theorized that increased exports will lead to economic growth and thus impact economic development for increased gross domestic product. In pursuance thereof, measures such as business incentives, investment promotion, free zones enclaves, tax holidays, profit retention, and export promotion were introduced by various governments aimed at attracting foreign direct investment. It is again theorized that export-based industrial models will facilitate increased job creation.

For far too long, African governments have paid attention to large businesses capable of investing capital into their economies as against small business owners whose concentration is widespread and focused more on local needs. Once more, the end product of this philosophy is the increasing unemployment and widespread continental poverty. The lesson is that reliance on export-driven industrialization does not necessarily translate into wealth creation and improved living standards.

Challenges of the Export-Based Model

The associated challenges of the export-based model are the following;

- the emphasis is not on how productive people are in using local capital to generate higher income and thus increase their living standards, but that wealth is created by exporting goods and services to other countries. It ignores the fact that humans (with innovation to create wealth) are at the center of economic development, not only the quantum of wealth of a country;

- the goods and services produced are not for local consumption, hence incapable of meeting local needs. The locality would have to look elsewhere for them and spend their money, which consequently leaves the area, and by so doing, renders the economy vulnerable to external shocks;

- there is capital flight as these large companies transfer returns to their foreign owners, who might not even spend their money in the economy (where they invested) but in a different place. This is an unfortunate case for Africa since, roughly, the equivalent of US$ 50 billion is flown out of the continent annually. That amount could have increased development in many areas; and

- the relevance and the roles of other sectors of the economy, such as education, transport, health, roads, telecommunication, and security, are downplayed and classified as support services. But without them, businesses will not strive, and the quality of life cannot improve.

It is worth recalling that the economy of many African countries, despite the talk about open market and private sector being the engine of growth is characterized by:

- centralized economic decision-making powers with limited private sector participation;
- centrally driven strategies and interventions (top-down);
- public institutions that directly provide services and are de-concentrated to the regions and localities;
- a huge injection of economic capital into public institutions to the disadvantage of the private sector, civil society, and labor unions;
- excessive attention/incentives to large and medium scale industries against micro and small businesses;

- insignificant functional power and resources in the hands of local authorities to assume control of the economic direction in their jurisdictions; and
- inadequate local entrepreneurial skills.

African leaders have not taken the bold steps that will effectively change the direction of their economies away from the inherited colonial one. They rely on unprocessed goods such as minerals (gold, diamond, iron ore, copper, etc.) and agricultural products (cocoa, shea nut, cashew, and palm oil). Statistics by World Integrated Trade Solutions (2018) show that roughly USD121b worth of goods were exported in 2016 against imports of USD161b by Sub-Saharan countries. Cumulatively, Africans' share of the global export trade keeps dipping year in, year out, and there is no certainty that it will improve anytime soon because other countries/continents have laid a strong foundation to dominate and sustain their competitiveness on the world market.

The export market shows that the prices of processed goods are always pegged higher than unprocessed ones. Some economic analysts (for example, Honest Accounts Report: 2014) say that Africa would be roughly $119 billion richer if it had the same share of world exports in the 1980s. The "lost" money is estimated to be approximately five times the quantum of aid received. It explains why Africa gets lesser returns and has no control over the determination of the prices, including those for its goods. That hurts, and should be the motivation for African governments to plan their economies focusing on consumption patterns and also, support indigenous capital investment. Unless investment by Africans is boosted in the respective economies, it will be herculean to achieve an early economic empowerment.

Transfer of Technology

The transfer of technology should be a core demand in granting concessions to foreign investors in the economies of African countries. Experience has shown that loans, grants, credits, aid, and austerity measures have not significantly impacted livelihood. But when technology is in-house, Africans can transform their lives without depending fully on external entities. This shift in policy will not be without struggles since it will not readily serve the interests of the outside world.

Therefore, a continental strategy to mobilize, and invest in priority areas of technology, engineering, and vocational skills, within a broader industrialization framework should be in place. There should be budget targets for African governments to meet within agreed timelines. Partnership and joint country efforts should be encouraged to maximize returns but not to over-burden the economies of member countries. The ultimate is to rebrand Africa and make it a big player in the world market.

Diaspora Drive

One of the greatest assets of Africa in modern days is the pool of descendants, affiliates, sympathizers, identifiable groups, and professionals located in all parts of the developed world. It is an opportunity for progress, but the challenge is that African leaders are weak in the attempts to integrate them into the continental development agenda. It is about time that people living in the diaspora play a more befitting role beyond the festivals, monuments, and reminders of the slave trade. African leaders should search, build a database, and create a seat for them, especially at the continental and country-specific levels. The Diasporas have what many Africans lack; exposure, discipline, and assertiveness. When they heed the clarion call and re-dedicate themselves to work for the continent, the pace of development will be faster.

Public Sector Re-Engineering

The genesis and evolution of the public sector is not enabling for a new Africa. The colonial masters built it not to facilitate development but as a vessel to take away from the people, invest elsewhere, and without doubt, to make it answerable to no African. Above all, it was jam-packed with low-skilled workers who did not have the strategic mind to build and manage the complex system of statecraft, public policy, and service delivery. After independence and under the watch of politicians and managers, many state enterprises (except in very few countries) collapsed, and services became aborted. Its capacity to facilitate the private sector as the engine of growth is equally challenging because it is not readily responsive to the prevailing dynamism of business. There have been externally driven attempts at reforms without much productive gains since the sector remains managed like a project without any serious identification of crosscutting issues and linkages to the national development agenda. All said and done, the public sector, in its current form is not enabling for new African leaders to use and lift up the people.

One may ask, what is the public sector, and what is it required to do? Unlike Western democracy, which recognizes the sector as independent from the Executive, rules-based, and accountable for its action (to secure the mission and integrity of the State and the people), many African countries put it in the throes of the Executive Arm of government, and use it as a rubber stamp institution.

Unlike Western democracy, which protects public servants against political vagaries, the sector is vulnerable and unable to act courageously in Africa. In contrast to the West where employment is based strictly on the merit system, it is not so in Africa. The Western system has an enabling condition of service that guarantees decent livelihood of workers, but the same cannot be said for Africa. The major professional challenges of the public sector include:

- how to properly situate it to be answerable for its actions without any ex-ante controls from the various arms of government, especially the Executive;
- how it should protect the public purse while serving as the means for executing policies of the government in power;
- how to make it performance-based, delivering on the policy

of the government and at the same time responding to its constitutional requirement to serve the State but not political and individual interest; and

- how to reduce waste, corruption, and poor working attitudes. Perhaps the level of resource waste in the public sector outweighs (if not the same) the level of corruption.

The Neo-African leader needs to be conversant with the Constitution, and the structures and processes of the public sector. Unfortunately, many leaders never took time off to study the workings of the public sector and ended up weakening it or frustrating the very means by which they are to deliver on their campaign promises and policies.

Leaders should know what they want the public sector to be in their development agenda. Is it to;

   i. protect the State and the Constitution?
  ii. secure the rights, freedoms, and responsibilities of citizens?
 iii. be independent yet accountable in the execution of policy decisions?
 iv. deliver responsive and quality services (directly or indirectly) to the citizens?

Modern-day democracy and institution-building demand that all these features should be proportionally integral to it. The leader should decide how to blend them. It means that for the new African leader, the independence of the public sector (structure and processes spelt out in law and administrative policies), should be protected, and, at the same time, it should be held accountable for its actions. Similarly, it should recruit highly skilled people, with the capacity to think strategically, having the zeal, and experience to deliver quality policies and services.

Governance Re-Arrangement

Has multi-party democracy come to stay in Africa? Will it facilitate rapid development on the continent? It is important to note that nowhere in the literature has it been concluded that multi-party democracy is the surest way to rapid development. Otherwise, how could China develop so quickly to be where it is today? The multi-party system, as practiced currently, sends some worrying signals. It is characterized by:

- winner takes all;
- monetization of votes;
- stifling of the opposition party;
- the dominance of elites;
- heavy handedness of party in government against opposition parties;
- unfair distribution of resources; a system that makes it possible for the wealthy to get more and without paying their fair share to the State;
- intra and inter-party conflicts to the point that the national agenda is seen through party lenses;
- dividing society along party lines;
- excessive power to the incumbent;
- relegating or abandoning programs and projects of previous governments;
- centralized decision-making;
- abuse of incumbency;
- low level of transparency and accountability, especially in the award of contracts and use of public resources;
- manipulation of public institutions by central government;
- low public trust in Electoral Commissions;
- shirking of civic responsibility;
- break down in discipline;
- weak popular participation; and
- overall, widespread poverty.

These factors impede efforts to build a progressive Africa. The irony is that when a party is in opposition, it continually cries foul and acts as if it has the best answers, but when it assumes power, it becomes silent on the issues or tend to repeat (if not worse) the same wrongs. The driving force in office seems to be how to amass wealth before the next election. Sadly, all this wrongs are perpetuated by the literate class, the imitators of Western democracy while the ordinary African stands helpless, wondering what is happening and whether politicians can ever be trustworthy.

So, if leaders (no matter which party they belong to) do not extoll and live the noble virtues of democracy, where does Africa go, and what are the answers? It may be that democracy is good, but multi-party democracy is inappropriate for Africa at this stage of development. The weight of this statement depends on how well African leaders conduct themselves and build democratic institutions towards societal progress.

Reconstruction of African Leadership

Having inherited the Western governance model, African governments have no choice but to practice it by the book. The State at the national level comprises the Executive, Judiciary, and Legislature. The Press is the 4th organ. The inherent challenge in this arrangement is the extent of separation of powers. In many countries, so much power is vested in the President at the national level that it forecloses those who work at the regional and local levels. One will think that the separation of powers should be at multi-territorial, multi-sector, and multi-stakeholder levels so that strategic decisions for national cohesion, defense and international cooperation will be matters of primary concern and authority at the central government level, while day-to-day livelihood issues will be handled more at the sub-national level. Of course, national level institutions should be more focused on policy initiatives, coordination and outcomes. When so much power (including livelihood matters) is directly vested in the President at the central level, structural defects, irresponsive decisions and lack of good governance quality in a leader will hinder the fierce action for development.

The structural arrangement of the state in many African countries includes regional and local governments, which are the instruments for exercising democratic rights and development at the sub-national level. As often proclaimed by governance theorists, the people have the right to participate in decisions that affect their living conditions. There is therefore, the need to strengthen local and regional participation across African countries, not only in popular elections but in decisions that bother on livelihood. In effect, resources should be progressively increased to local and regional levels backed by robust checks and balances. It is difficult at times to appreciate the development need addressed at the national level when so much resources are in the hands of centralized institutions. Often, they undertake activities that do not impact the well-being of citizens but to maintain themselves as institutions. The microcosm or the building block of democracy is at the individual, family, and community levels where the goods and services are needed and should be delivered. By so doing, the national or continental economic empowerment could be measured.

Unfortunately, many African leaders have not given adequate attention to the micro levels. Markedly, the generation of elderly African leaders, who were born in the pre and early post-independence period is about to end. The new crop of leaders will be those who were born after independence, whose leadership ethos are likely going to be more aligned to the dynamics of today's world. They should draw lessons from the past to reinvigorate governance, administrative, and socio-economic issues. The lessons should give them a deeper understanding of the continental issues so that they could be more forthright in policy actions. In any case, they have the benefit of some enabling factors which could be used to improve living conditions on the continent. These are;

i. the world has seen the strengths of the Americas, Asians,

Europeans, Middle East and others, but that of Africa is yet to unravel. The continent is the last sleeping giant on earth. Many countries all over the world rely on her resources. The incidence of indebtedness, capital flight, aid, grants, conditionality, austerity measures, trade barriers, and bad deals, are but temporary and can be transformed into positive action. Africa can extricate herself by decisiveness, maturity, resource internalization, and the will to be free from external controls through relationship renewal with the world. The guiding philosophy is that Africa's innocence should no longer be misinterpreted as ignorance.

ii. the continent is the second most populous after Asia. Its population of 1.2 billion (in 2016) will likely double by 2045. It has the benefit of being the youngest population; the median age was 19.7 in 2012 against 38.3 world median. Therefore, leaders should put in concerted efforts to transform this catalytic asset into a rich human resource by equipping people to become more intelligent, well-exposed, and hardworking. With the proper facilitation, there is no reason for Africans not to be well-positioned to compete with people from other parts of the world. A bright future beckons, and unbelievable moments await the continent.

iii. the use of technology, from the olden days, has always led to increased production. That is the strength of the developed world. The excess production of goods and services demands new markets, and Africa has always been a responsive consumer all this years. Wealth in the developed countries is the reciprocal contribution of Africans - without it many developed countries will flounder. Imagine that for a moment, Africans decide to put the demand for foreign goods on hold (or develop substitutes) or reduce the export of primary goods, surely, there will be economic problems throughout the world. Whereas people of the continent have options, other countries that depend on Africa hardly have any options.

Westerners are used to a lifestyle that they term "advanced" and cannot withstand a fraction of the hardship Africans have endured for centuries. Foreign governments know it, and that is why they will always keep their eyes on the economic balls, to maintain their advantages on the continent. Any change is bound to cause a dislocation and the need to make new deals with African governments. The outside world does not want that change and will find ways and means to influence the decisions. This situation, however contains the trump card which new African leaders should use wisely to break the external domination of resources on the continent. A weak leader cannot use the trump card to strike a better deal. It takes a strong negotiator to do so. Look at the US President's announcement in early 2018 to slap tariffs on China and European aluminum and steel imports to revive American industries. This is entrepreneurial regardless of the odds. Who, for once, will ever think that an American President could do that to "friends and foes"? It is not about being diplomatically nice and pretty. It is about the reality that lives should get better. An African leader who does not see any change in the living conditions of his people needs to take action in like manner and ACT with fierce URGENCY.

i.   Africa has an enormous land mass, the second largest on Earth estimated to be more than 30 million km^2. She has the largest uncultivated fertile lands and unlimited supplies of nature's gifts of life; varied climatic conditions (it is the only continent stretching from northern to southern hemispheres), home to the highest mineral reserves, has five countries among the world's top oil and gas producers, and unequaled oil reserves. Archaeologically, the first human species on Earth were found on the continent. Her exquisite natural vegetation includes evergreen forests, big lakes and rivers, abundant sunlight, captivating mountains, vast grasslands, flora, and faunas. She is home to a variety of animal and bird species. Most importantly, the natural wealth of Africa remains largely untapped, and many more are yet to be explored for tomorrow's industrial, technology, energy, infrastructural, and medical use. The whole continent is sitting on unmatched natural competitive wealth.

ii. a lot of the raw materials for manufacturing in developed countries come from Africa. There are cases where one raw material can be processed into several other products. Examples include cocoa, shea nuts, cashews, coffee, gold, diamond, iron ore, and copper whose by-products are even tradeable. The external control of African commodity prices and the low prices on the world market are regrettable. The old way should go. So, leaders through the AU or affiliate bodies should send signals of a movement away from the existing unfavorable terms of trade to a demand for re-negotiation. A uniform continental approach will create more wins for Africa than a single-country approach which has been in use from the colonial days without any profitable results. The attempt to reset terms of trade should be "forcefully" stated, loudly, and repeatedly like "The Donald' does anytime his anticipated change simmered.

The world will continue to come to Africa. An adage says, "A good product with a monopoly does not have to worry itself about marketing; the customers will come." The advancement of the world is still a work in progress, and competition in geo-political ideology aided by free trade is advantageous to Africa. Foreign governments and businesses from the west to the east, and from the south to the north will have to keep knocking at the doors of Africa. They will come in search of resources, to build friendships, and above all, to have a foothold on the continent. It is no fluke that foreign direct investment is increasing and Africa is performing well on the list of the world's fast-growing economies year by year. Since many countries will need the continent, Africans should welcome them all, as has been the practice from time immemorial. The people of the continent have always been welcoming to all societies, showing love and ready for partnership towards the progress of humanity. But this time, African leaders should avoid any blind trusting relationship; they should be assertive and set the terms of engagement because they have the trump card.

The reconstruction of African leadership calls for deeper intra-continental collaboration, mentoring, and standards setting. It means leadership training programs (practically linked to immediate environment) should be integral to curriculum, targeting not just anybody but people who have the potential to lead in various capacities. Progressively, Africans will produce a cream of leaders to drive the continental development agenda forward.

Western Versus African Governance Model

The leadership work to harvest prosperity for Africans is heavy. There are intricacies that bother on how to build political, governance, and institutional structures, processes, and ownership. It is no gainsaying that the Western political arrangement at the national level is distant and alien to the true identity of Africans. That arrangement works for some literates but not for the masses who paradoxically are said to have sovereignty of the state. The attempt to educate them on the national governance arrangement, civic responsibility, and liberties are not yielding expected results.

In the local areas, the average African knows from childhood who is the traditional authority, his powers, the consequences of breaking societal values, norms, and ethics. He lives by the admonition of his parents regarding good neighborliness. The effect of his conduct is not seen as exclusive to him but cascades on the whole extended family. This awareness influences him to become a responsible community member. Indeed, the power of tradition speaks to the hearts and minds of Africans right from birth, deeply rooted in the DNA, and bonds members to their communities. The colonial attempts to crush it failed. It is, therefore, pathetic that leaders at the national level have failed over the years to invest in its strength for an all-inclusive locality management and development.

Some African leaders even labored to undermine traditional institutions. They accused them of being ethnically biased, uneducated, non-democratic, archaic, out-of-touch, and overly materialistic. Is it not disheartening for politicians to steamroll these allegations when they (i.e. politicians) have done and continue to do more grievous things? They (politicians) by far, have corrupted the sovereignty of the people by insincerity, falsehood, mediocrity, monetization of office, and unabashed corruption. Many hold the view that they have so contaminated politics in Africa that their conscience should purge them if they care to reflect. Their actions undermined the ethos of the independence struggle, which, for all intent and purpose, was not to exploit the people but to make them competitive and happy in line with their cultural identity.

In the face of political leadership failures, people feel that there has to be a remaking of the African politician, especially those with western orientation, who unfortunately, are deemed not to be well-rounded enough to appreciate the enormity of the African developmental challenges. The feeling is that their orientation was not any different from the old educational system by which the "African-by-Nature and

European-by-Nurture" exploited his fellows to live a comfortable material life.

In retrospect, the agitation against the traditional governance system was not carried out by the Europeans. It was the seduction the indoctrinated literate African offered his people - to eventually lead them in the image of colonial masters. He failed in his quest to see that building a strong multi-level governance arrangement creates ownership and yields faster results for the people than having a cloistered political system at the top that works largely for the literate.

Meanwhile, the governance arrangement built by the Europeans was not a fluke; a lot of strategic thinking went into it for sustainability. It was for good reason that some colonialists adopted the indirect rule. They knew the essence of socio-cultural and political stability to trade and commerce. Hence, they took steps to formalize and strengthen the existing traditional governance system. Take a look at Ghana, for example; the British passed many ordinances to give certain positions and roles to traditional leaders at both local and regional levels. Their functions included maintenance of law and order, public health, customary matters, passing bye-laws (including healthy sanitation practices and environment protection), raising revenues, et cetera. Thus the chiefs were empowered to administer localities based on the prevailing traditional and customary laws in their jurisdiction.

By this arrangement, communities continued to relate to the governance system they were ushered into from birth. Sadly, the educated Africans opposed the existing order and made strong cases before the colonial masters for reforms. The underlying intention was to moderate the power of the chiefs and, eventually, scheme themselves into power. Indeed, they succeeded after independence and without holding back, reduced traditional authorities, in many cases, to ceremonial and religious figure heads. They then went ahead and built their local government systems around European models that empowered the class of "African-by-Nature and European-by-Nurture" to perform leadership roles. Meanwhile, the appointed or elected politicians have little influence in their communities. They are seen as local leaders by position with only a handful of genuine followers. The vast majority of the people continue to adhere to the traditional order.

At the national level, the motivation of the "African-by-Nature and European-by- Nurture" was to capture political power by whatever means possible. He was unsung and could not fathom or prioritize building of strong governance institutions. There were no serious plans or commitments to attend to the needs of the people excepting the pride, greed, and self-esteem. For the "African by Nature and European-by-Nurture," politics is business, a means to livelihood, comfort, and the big things of life. The misunderstanding of "politics" at the national level has wrecked many lives for far too long. The penchant to win power at all cost has dire consequences. It is the cause of many post-independence wars on the continent, from Liberia to Sierra Leone, from Ivory Coast to Kenya among others. Africa has not seen any traditional authorities waging or stoking wars for political power on the scale that the adulterated literates did.

It is apparent that imitating the Western political system is easier for the "African-by-Nature and European-by-Nurture," but translating it into a governance arrangement that works and is conducive for the people is elusive. No one should expect the West or Asians to do it for Africa; it is the responsibility of Africans to design their system and show the rest of the world that, indeed, governance can also be built be on the African Personality which sprouts from culture and frowns on individualization. It is grounded in family and social cohesiveness, tolerance of others, and integration of ideas. It allows for a repositioning in tandem with modern trends without uprooting the underlying tenets and values of tradition. Its style is unique and can become the bedrock of regional and local governance. When properly aligned and applied, it can project Africans to earning respect and a befitting place in the world.

By analogy it stands to reason that since it was by dislodging the traditional system that Africans became "lost", by the same token, Africans will reclaim their God-given happy life when the traditional system is revitalized. That is to say, the reconstruction of the continent's governance system particularly at the local levels will be the gateway to the restoration of the African personality. Therefore, there should be concerted efforts to build strong traditional institutions to work hand in hand with state institutions at the national, regional and local levels – where their authority will be limited to their jurisdictional areas with emphasis on clarity of roles and resource allocation.

The one-sided, over-reliance on the Western governance model is bare without tangible value-laden results for the people because it does not speak to the inner being of the African. When new leaders reinvigorate the traditional system to partner state institutions on terms of equality, Africans will be well positioned to utilize governance products on a higher scale of transparency and accountability. It is an equalizing factor that has been absent since the literate Africans took over the reins of governance. The blend will see both State Institutions and Traditional Authority working hand in hand for the African, a long yearning that will possibly harmonize the conflict within/between the "African-by-Nature" and the "European-by-Nurture."

By so doing, the old-long dream of a turnaround in the tribulations of colonialism would have been fulfilled. The African Personality would reemerge and get stronger through renewal. The people of the continent will become more competitive and grander on the world stage, and above all, the slavery days would have found a more permanent reparation. The next generations will learn about the African renaissance and be proud of those who worked it out. Who can make this happen? No single individual can but building a new leadership movement across the continent is the trump card.

CHAPTER SIX

Moral Conviction and Action

The making of great nations does not lie only in the appearance of massive infrastructure and a buoyant business but in the intrinsic commitment to values, ethics, and morality that bind people together for progress. A society that does not uphold and foster what is good and just for people to do stands bedeviled by developmental challenges, chief among them being deficits in living conditions. The rich will get richer while the poor will get poorer as leaders pay lip service to development and prioritize materiality and self-aggrandizement. Consequentially, a degenerative cycle of poverty will prevail to compromise efforts at ensuring a happy life for everybody.

A leadership hoisted on high moral grounds is the panacea to the numerous developmental challenges. But when it matters most, many African leaders falter because their motivation hinges on the adage "power first, and all other things shall be added." They are ill-prepared to navigate the moral entrapments of democracy from a bouquet of push and pull factors.

1. *Appointments*: There is enough room for a leader to exercise discretion about who serves in his government. Aside from the constitutional and statutory eligibility criteria, the leader has a set of additional qualities to sieve potential candidates. To what extent will he highlight qualification, competence, and experience? Will he succumb to favoritism, ethnicity, familiarity, and loyalty? There are many cases across Africa where leaders appoint family members, friends, and cronies to sensitive public positions. Examples include Ghana (2017-2024), Togo (1967-2024), and Gabon (1967-2023). The argument is put up in defense that the favored appointees are also citizens whose rights should not be curtailed merely

because of their relationship with the leader. That is a simplistic view of the matter. The issues of morality and the strain of courage that the leader needs to surmount to sanction is enormous. The danger is that if they get implicated, the case will be manipulated or swept under the carpet. The leader becomes vulnerable and likely to compromise ethical principles by bending the rules to protect them. So, the safer way to go is to apply the technique of avoidance-avoidance by not offering them front rower positions.

2. *Party interest versus national interest*: Generally, leaders emerge from political parties that remain relevant throughout the tenure of the President. They are the means for contesting future elections. Thus, the decisions made by the Presidency are not exclusive to the national interest but also consider party interest. In some situations, decisions that inure to the national interest may not receive a premium because there is no cascading effect on the gains of the party in power. It takes a courageous leader to manage these competing interests for the common good.

3. *Internal party cohesion*: The African leader hardly makes decisions without looking at favorability to party unity. Considerations such as party philosophy, mission, values, and prospects in the next elections inform policy decisions and interventions. So, if a policy is laudable and appropriate to governance trends, leaders find it challenging to adapt if it does not fit readily into or promote party unity. In similar cases, juicy contracts and favors are primed towards enriching party members and executives regardless of their capacity to deliver on the job satisfactorily. Where there are infractions by party members and loyalists, African leaders find it difficult to uphold fairness and the rule of law such that they are prone to interfering with the justice system or appoint favorites who

are ever willing and pliable to stall outcomes of investigations and set the "culprits" free.

4. *Spread of development projects*: The call to ensure national and regional balance in the spread of development programs and projects is a constitutional demand on many African governments. However, the allocation of resources, especially from the central/national government to many parts of the country, in many cases lacks a clear scientific basis to fulfil the requirement. Political promises become the determinant, and areas that give the ruling government more votes stand tall in the distribution of resources to the marginalization of opposition areas.

5. *Personal interest and security on leaving office*: Political power is sweet, and it is just human to wish to be in power as long as possible. Since the constitution stipulates a tenure of office, many African leaders would want to maintain the lifestyle they had while in office. It is a thorny moral entrapment because the conditions of service of a president cannot guarantee and secure that desired living standard. So, while in office, they put energy into securing in advance the comforts of good living that they desire. They create opportunities and scheme through cronies who front for them and carry out their wishes.

6. *Winning the next election and financing*: The ultimate goal of political parties is to win elections and come into office to implement their vision. Ruling governments would like to remain in power as long as it takes. Thus, raising resources has been at the center of policy decision-making. New policies and interventions are inherently meant to create financial opportunities for party followers. The award of contracts has unofficial injunctions; aside from contract awards to party followers (mostly, by single-sourcing), there is also a "hidden

push" for a certain percentage of the contract sum to be given to the party.

7. How to satisfy varied competitive interests within and outside government.

8. How to live by party ideology in the face of the dynamism of time.

9. How to hold appointees responsible for performance. Will it be strictly performance-based or a blend of formality and informality?

10. *Managing the influence of family, friends, and acquaintances*: Many people think that an African leader should use his position to solve the financial and economic problems of his immediate and remote family members and acquaintances. It is almost abominable if he objects to abusing his office in such a manner. In the wake of a weak (i) merit system (ii) transparency, and (iii) accountability, many African leaders lost their moral grounds and succumbed to the wishes of relatives and friends.

11. *Contracts and the pecuniary of office*: Many incentives form part of the office of the leader. Will the leader accept gifts and other influence-peddling offers? In the absence of a clear-cut ethical standards and values, many African leaders have the discretion to do as they think fit, regardless of the morality of their decision.

12. Managing Fall-Outs. There is hardly any government that does not have fall-outs from disagreements over issues, interests, and resource allocations. Several leaders find it hard to manage their teams because of weak principles, improper orientation, and lack of exemplary leadership style.

Internal Issues: The multi-ethnic diversity of people with peculiar historical antecedents poses a challenge to the African leader. Even though there is some commonality in traditional and cultural practices, many areas of the country have unique practices, values, and interests. Some ethnic groups stereotyped themselves as superior to others. Unfortunately, many countries have not taken steps to make laws that will outlaw derogatory remarks and abuse of any ethnic group. The leader should be conversant with this diversity and act not to incur the displeasure of any section of the people. The more challenging issue is how to endear himself to opposition areas of the country, who, no matter how well he does in office, are likely going to remain as they are, unchanged.

External Issues: The international environment has become very complex, fluid, and fast-changing. The issues and positions adopted some years ago have become obsolete due to geo-politics. There has been a surge in building new alliances. The philosophical foundation established by past leaders is under siege and demands the African leader to find a balance between now and the future. In the attempt to do so, juicy offers are often made by foreign governments, multi-lateral corporations, lobbyists, and influence peddlers to have an advantage over other parties. The competing demands should be well-managed, and it requires strong moral courage from the African leader to make a just and guided decision that should stand the test of time

The effective leader should not limit himself to only the acquisition of knowledge about what is morally right and ethical but should also have the audacity to (i) stand for the right (ii) make hard decisions against all odds, and (iii) practice what is for the common good. The outcome of the choices may be positive or negative in the immediate to the long term. Accordingly, the African leader should meticulously navigate the moral maze for answers. Any decision that primes itself on self, party, or ethnic interest is in opposition to sound morality, and to avoid that, the leader should set his ethical standards in tandem with the culture, tradition, and constitutional framework.

Bibliography

CNN Marketplace Africa; https://www.youtube.com/watch?v=s6CaHEyN9N8 on 4/02/17.

cnn.com (2018), https://edition.cnn.com/videos/politics/2018/06/21/trump-more-elite-than-the-elites-haberman-newday.cnn

Donald Trump (2016), Acceptance Speech of at Republican Convention, 18-21 July, 2016, Cleveland, USA.

Donald Trump (2017), Inaugural Address, 20th January, 2017, Washington D.C. USA

Donald Trump (2017), Address at the UN General Assembly on 19th September, 2018, New York, USA.

Honest Accounts Report (2014), The true story of Africa's billion dollar losses, UK.

Grinker, R. R, Lubkemann S. C., Steiner C.B. (2010), Perspectives on Africa: A reader in culture, history and representation, (2nd Ed.), Wiley-Blackwell, UK.

Integrated Trade Solutions (https://wits.worldbank.org/CountryProfile/en/SSF 26th April 2018.

James Harvey Robinson (1908), An Introduction to the History of Western Europe,

Fustel De Coulanges Ginn & Company, Boston.

Kwame Nkrumah (1962), Address at the Conference of African Freedom Fighters in Accra, 4th June, 1962.

Learry Gagné; *A Modern Interpretation of Machiavelli's Political Cycle* Canadian Political Science Review, Vol. 5, No. 2, 2011, 127-135.

The Planning Committee of the AU Arts Festival (2018), Statement to mark 2018 AU Day under the theme: "Winning the Fight against Corruption: A Sustainable Path to Africa's Transformation", Accra.

wikipedia.org/wiki/DonaldTrumpWorld[1].

---

1.   https://en.wikipedia.org/wiki/Donald_TrumpWorld

Don't miss out!

Visit the website below and you can sign up to receive emails whenever Scddoh Bokor publishes a new book. There's no charge and no obligation.

https://books2read.com/r/B-A-DNMY-SQOID

BOOKS 2 READ

Connecting independent readers to independent writers.

Did you love *Movement of New African Leaders*? Then you should read *The Second Betrayal of Jesus Christ*[2] by Seddoh Bokor!

[3]

The Synoptic Gospels recount how material desires influenced Judas Iscariot to betray Jesus Christ with a traitorous kiss. Thence, he became a religious reference point for sinful conduct. But could there be more to it than literally interpreted? How does the story apply to the spiritual development of those who profess to be Christians? This book is about religion and science. It disagrees with the popular notion that there is a turf war between them and gives weight to the deeper meanings of the Christian Bible and how they connect to science. It provides spiritual explanation of scriptures that relate to scientific conclusions about the universe, galaxies, solar systems, etc. and how

---

2. https://books2read.com/u/mVDRlJ

3. https://books2read.com/u/mVDRlJ

humanity is connected as a citizen. It throws light on the all-important question of whether human beings are alone in the observable universe.

The book goes beyond the literal explanation of the Bible and brings to the reader, mindboggling revelations of the deeper teachings of the Christian Religion - from Genesis to Revelation - which have been in circulation in secret places for ages and the loop of enlightened individuals. It explains the material and spiritual journey of humanity whilst 'decoding' the cabalistic expressions of Adam and Eve, Garden of Eden, Fall of Man, Noachian Flood, Tabernacle in the Wilderness, Trinity, Christ and Jesus of Nazareth, Saving Grace, and End Time.

The book emphasizes the dangers of attachment to materiality which include the betrayal of Jesus Christ, and subsequent deprivation of the individual from building the spiritual body which the class of advanced human beings will use in the future on a transformed Earth beyond the exigencies of physical body, water, oxygen, gravity, distance, time, marriage, sickness, and death.